I commend to you Amber Massey and  porates her love for horses, her love for [...] the Lord in a mighty way.

—Dr. Frank S. [...] [...]utive officer,
Southern B[...] [...]tion Executive Committee

Amber's vision of reaching the equestrian community with her personal stories of growing, learning, and overcoming is remarkable. I know this book will reach many hands and touch many hearts.

—Carolyn Culbertson, 2011–2013 district commissioner,
Greenville Foothills Pony Club

The challenge of cowboy and equestrian ministry is to find material that teaches biblical truth from the perspective of those cultures. Amber Massey has accomplished just that in this book. You feel you are living each adventure along with Amber and her horse, Marquise. Each chapter drives home an important biblical lesson, and I recommend this book for all who love the cowboy way, animals of all sorts—especially horses—or just the great outdoors.

—W. Douglas Davis, pastor, Triad Cowboy Church,
Archdale, North Carolina

Amber Massey's equestrian stories are truly heartwarming. The bond between horse and rider is delicate and unique, and Amber creates a vivid depiction of trust and security on the trail of life. Her devotion as a Christ follower permeates the essays and glorifies the Creator of all things.

—Kelley Phillips, DVM, Cleveland Park Animal Hospital,
Travelers Rest, South Carolina

As professionals in the horse business, we've met thousands of people who share a passion for one of God's most magnificent creations—the horse. In these compilations, Amber sets herself apart from and relates to all horse lovers by writing with heart, passion, and love for God. Amber inspires us to learn about ourselves as we learn about and tend to our horses. We are honored to be part of this project.

—Eric Dierks and **Trayce Doubek-Dierks,** trainers, owners, and operators,
Dierks Equestrian and Renovatio Farms in Tryon, North Carolina

For *the* Love *of* Horses

AMBER H. MASSEY

HARVEST HOUSE PUBLISHERS
EUGENE, OREGON

Cover by Left Coast Design, Portland, Oregon

Front and back cover photos by Bonnie Hill of Bonnie McGhee Photography, www.myimagesbybonnie.com

FOR THE LOVE OF HORSES
Copyright © 2014 Amber H. Massey
Published by Harvest House Publishers
Eugene, Oregon 97402
www.harvesthousepublishers.com

Library of Congress Cataloging-in-Publication Data
    Massey, Amber H., 1976-
    For the love of horses / Amber H. Massey.
      pages cm
    ISBN 978-0-7369-5822-6 (pbk.)
    ISBN 978-0-7369-5823-3 (eBook)
    1. Human-animal relationships. 2. Horses. I. Title.
    QL85.M316 2014
    636.1—dc23

                                    2013043563

To anyone who has ever endured for the love of a horse.

Special Thanks

There are many people whose love and encouragement have been the strength behind this book, and to them I say thank you...

- to Jeff for finally saying yes to my dream of owning a horse and for loving, supporting, and funding our animal family.

- to my family. Looks like the horse craze never went away. Thanks for loving me through it.

- to Erin for transforming a notebook full of really bad grammar into something worth reading.

- to my friends who have allowed me to share their stories and horses with the world.

- to all the veterinarians and their technicians who have cared for Marquise and me.

- to Harvest House for believing in the value of using horses to share Christ's love.

Contents

Then and Now

It seems like only yesterday that Marquise and I were learning the ins and outs of endurance riding and looking forward to a very bright future on the trail. Riding for hours at a time was a passion, and it didn't matter whether I was competing, training, or just enjoying a brisk fall afternoon.

After only a few short years of trail riding over so many wonderful miles, Marquise's career came to an abrupt end, and in light of his early retirement, my identity as an equestrian felt phony. Hay, dirt, leather, and riding consumed me for so long that I began to grasp at anything for fulfillment. Thankfully, I picked up a pen and paper and wrote.

Little stories, life lessons—devotions if you will—began to form, and God's desire became clear.

Some equestrians like me seek to connect with greatness and strive to fill this need by obtaining oneness with a horse, but this satisfaction lasts only until the tack is hung. Much greater and longer lasting joy is found in an intimate relationship with Christ. Even though I longed to be in the saddle, the time I spent carefully listening to God was worth the sacrifice and opened my eyes to some valuable truths.

The first truth is that my purpose is to imitate Christ and selflessly follow Him. God's plan was for me to write a book that would speak to horse lovers, but He knew my desire to ride stood in the way of my wholehearted focus. By allowing riding to be temporarily removed from my life, I was able to concentrate on God's desire rather than my own.

The second is this. For now Christ has called me to write. Rather than using my time to ride, He's asked me to invest in others and reach out to those who share my unbridled love for horses. For those of you who are out there riding, do so with vigor and enjoy the blessing of knowing that until He calls you to do something else, you're good right where you are.

When Marquise galloped down the trail to early retirement, my purpose changed. I went from being an aspiring endurance rider to a writer, yet God was gracious and added a new equestrian identity. Marquise is now trail sound, and I'm amazed how God puts people in my path to love on. Who I am now is different than what I would have expected, but in this new season of life, I'm able to have some really wonderful conversations out in the quiet of the woods.

"The chosen fishermen weren't chosen because they were the best, but they were chosen because they were willing to cast their nets."

Pastor Paul Jimenez

1

Diamond in the Rough

A horse. It was all I ever *really* wanted. Every birthday, Christmas, and Easter, I dreamed of waking up and finding that special pony happily munching grass in our suburban front yard.

Through the years I was content with Barbie horses, horse sleeping bags, horse calendars, and horse-themed birthday parties. I carefully saved and rolled the coins from my allowance so that when I had saved enough, I could buy another Breyer and add it to the collection already filling my room. For a very long time, I dreamed of owning my first *real* horse and knew that when the time was right, everything would be perfect.

Twenty-eight years old and armed with a well-planned budget, I presented my childhood dream to my husband, Jeff. He'd heard my argument before and never agreed, but this time his answer was different. It was yes, but as the self-proclaimed family-pet-namer, he had one stipulation—he wanted to name the next member of our animal family.

Naming a horse isn't a right. It's a privilege, and the chosen name should reflect the horse's character and honor. I knew there was going to be further discussion about this, but that conversation could wait until after four hooves were firmly planted in my pasture.

When Jeff told me he'd picked out the name Huckleberry, my mind flashed to pictures of Doc Holliday in *Tombstone*. My skin crawled at the thought, but arguing was useless. What I really wanted was a horse, and as long as a yes still lingered on Jeff's lips, I wasn't going to push the naming issue.

My childhood snuck up on me, and I rolled every loose coin I could find around the house. Maria and Theresa, my dear friends, enthusiastically joined the search for my dream horse. Thanks to those two, my in-box was never without pictures of a new possibility one of them had found.

When searching for the perfect partner to share life's miles with, getting caught up in the moment and buying a horse that may not be your best match is easy. So I deliberately created two lists to review before making a purchase. One list was titled "Have-to-Have," and the other was titled "Hope-to-Have."

On my have-to-have list was an eight- to ten-year-old Arabian gelding who'd been there, done that. I wanted him to have enough spirit so we could have fun for years to come but enough experience to be a patient and willing teacher. Although good looks would be nice, they weren't a requirement. With a frown I bumped that trait onto the hope-to-have list.

My eyes blurred as I stared at the computer screen in front of me, so for a moment I took a break, leaned back, closed my eyes, and dreamed. I pictured myself astride my new equine friend with all the hope-to-haves a girl could want. His coat glistened, and his great hooves pounded the earth as we raced the sunset across fields of blazing red poppies. As nothing more than a silhouette, we rode until the South Carolina sun dipped beneath the horizon and night enveloped us in its quiet splendor.

Ugh. Shaking sense into my head, I remembered an old saying and a promise I made to myself. "Pretty is as pretty does." Good looks weren't going to get me down the trail and back in one piece. Have-to-haves had to come first.

Weeks into the search, I spent countless hours e-mailing sellers, looking at pictures, and traveling to several southern states. Early in my search, it became evident that I heavily leaned toward tall, muscular bays, but the three I'd gone to see didn't work out so well. The first cribbed, the second reared, and the third had a glimmer in his eye that told me he was not one to be trusted. Settling wasn't an option, but the more I looked and came up empty-handed, the more anxious I became to find *my horse.* He had to be out there somewhere, and with just a little more effort, perhaps I could find him. Frustration began to get the better of me.

One night I was up late tediously exploring the Internet again and clicked on a picture of a handsome chestnut with a flaxen mane. He was quite a looker, flashy on all accounts, and something about his attitude in the photo caught my eye. Always curious when I'd find my Huckleberry, Jeff poked his head in the room to offer encouragement. It only took him a minute to notice the pedigree of the little red horse. An equine scholar he is not, so he certainly didn't realize the weight of his statement when he said, "That's your horse. Make the call and go get him." All he knew was that the little red horse's grandsire was *Huckleberry* Bey.

Theresa and I rolled into the city limits of Bristol, Tennessee, within the week. A winding road meandered through the woods for a mile or so before it opened up and released us into the arms of a country estate with gently rolling hills and miles of pristine white fencing. Driving toward the farm, we couldn't help but blink hard after staring in amazement.

Ponds with banks of lush grass were dotted with ivory-colored swans. Great Pyrenees protectively patrolled the yard while watching their herds for any sign of unrest. As we neared the barn, I leaned forward in my seat, hoping to steal an early peek of *my horse.*

Directly ahead of us was a large pasture boasting horses of every size, shape, and color. They playfully tossed their heads and ran the fence in celebration of the new visitors. I caught sight of a few chestnuts basking in the sun, but based on their small size, they were much too young to be my horse. Continuing to scan my surroundings, I noticed a small pasture on my left with the homeliest bunch of horses I'd ever seen.

In contrast to the animated equines in the other paddock, these horses lazily wandered around picking at the grass or dozing beneath the canopy of shade trees. One chestnut in particular drew my attention. He stood alone, away from the group, and was obviously less than interested in the unfamiliar rig making its way up the driveway. Eyes half-closed and ears flopped in different directions indicated that he really didn't care what was going on. His rather large waistline and lack of conditioning were awkwardly accentuated as he stood with one leg cocking up his back end. My eyes took in the equine specimen before me, and I realized that cantering down a trail would be more than improbable with him. It would be impossible.

A chestnut's coat mirrors the sun and brilliantly reflects its red and gold rays. Sadly this little guy's coat was so caked in mud and rain rot that it reflected nothing more than the need for a bath and some serious TLC. Where the striking flaxen mane was supposed to hang, nothing more than a mass of tangled knots poked out erratically in every direction. Gone were his white socks. In their place were grass stains and burs. This horse was certainly the poster pony for some heavy-duty grooming products.

With a single gasp, I sucked all the air out of the truck, and Theresa shot a worried look my way. "I sure hope that's not him." The comment slipped from my lips as a whisper, but in my heart it was a desperate prayer.

Linda looked in the direction I was looking, and she quickly realized the cause of my concern. "There's *no* way Mr. Homely over there is Huckleberry Bey's grandson. I'm sure he's up in the barn already."

Sometimes prayers aren't answered the way we think they should be. After meeting the trainer at the barn, my heart sank as he led us down the path toward the homely horse pasture.

With a bucket of grain in hand, the trainer told us Mr. Homely's story. As the product of fine breeding, the little red horse was supposed to make it big in the show circuit. In his younger years, he had been shown in Halter, English Pleasure, and Native Costume Events, but due to the owner's financial difficulties, what began as a promising career had come to an abrupt halt. Now months later, Mr. Homely's value had dropped to whatever he could be sold for.

I trudged down the gravel path and barely lifted my eyes to give the tattered chestnut a second glance. The rocks at my feet had become increasingly interesting the more I lamented the time wasted seeing another dud. However, the scene drastically changed when the bucket of grain rattled.

Mr. Homely's eyes lit up. With a piercing call and thundering hooves, he raced past all the other horses coming our way. The gelding's tail proudly flew behind him as he approached at a full gallop that lasted only seconds and ended with a dramatic sliding stop. This time my gasp was a happy one as he pranced in tight circles and tossed his head with impatience.

There's my Huckleberry.

"We call him Marquise." The trainer grinned as he noticed me taking a second look at the now Not-So-Mr.-Homely, who somehow seemed to know he was going home with me that day. Marquise was certainly a mess, but I soon came to the realization that his name fit him perfectly. He was my diamond in the rough.

I'm sure Christ felt the same when He saw me. When I was lost and living a life of sin, I was covered with all sorts of ugliness and dirt. Content to lazily go through life the easy way, I didn't want to move outside of my comfort zone or put forth any extra effort.

When Jesus hung on the cross, He carried the weight of all my sins. It was so ugly that God had to turn His back. Looking at my shame was unbearable for such perfection. Just like I took Marquise home and gave him a bath, Jesus cleaned me up too. On the cross the price was paid for my sins and the sins of the world. By accepting this act of love, we can be washed as white as snow.

It's difficult to comprehend that no matter how sinful we are, Jesus is still willing and able to forgive us. Because we're human, when people sin against us, it can be hard to forget—even if we are able to forgive. Christ not only forgives us, but He also removes our sins. To Him it's as if our sins never happened.

> For as high as the heavens are above the earth, so great is his love for those who fear him; as far as the east is from the west, so far has he removed our transgressions from us.
>
> Psalm 103:11-12

Have you entered into a personal relationship with Jesus Christ that allows you to experience the freedom of unlimited love, forgiveness, and hope of eternal life? If you do not have a personal relationship with Jesus Christ, please consider making this step in your life.

Dear God, I understand that I am a sinner, and I know that without You in my life, I will remain hopelessly lost and unable to be spiritually clean. Thank You for Your Son, Jesus, who died on the cross to bear my sin and shame so that I may be forgiven. Send Your Holy Spirit to live in me so that I can begin a new life with You.

2

...Or You Can Sell Him

I've never seen a horse buck like that—and still haven't. I was in the saddle during the acrobatics and couldn't even claim to have been riding at the time. To Marquise I was nothing more than a fly he was trying to shake.

This was either the beginning of the end for Marquise and me, or *I* was going to learn to buck up.

⁘

When Theresa and I went to look at Marquise for the first time, she took the initial test ride. I watched and, of course, offered moral support. Cautiously watching for signs of protest, she stepped into the stirrup and swung her leg over. The saddle creaked in rhythm as they walked a few relaxed laps around the groomed arena before Theresa began to play with the bit, encouraging Marquise to stretch his neck and round his back.

And that he did.

Theresa obviously didn't like how *much* he rounded and quickly snatched his head back up.

"Oh, c'mon, Theresa. He's fine. Just let him drop his head," the trainer said, standing by the arena fence with his boot propped against the lowest board. He nodded toward the horse and rider and said to me, "He likes to do that. You know, reach down to stretch his back." Mr. Davidsen's opinion of how Marquise should be ridden was clear, and like most trainers do, he was going to make sure I knew it. But as the buyer, I trusted my friend.

Blonde curls bouncing, Theresa hopped off and held the reins out to me. "He's a nice ride, but the last time I felt that much roundness in a back was two seconds before Harley used me to play lawn darts. Keep his head up, and you'll be fine."

"That boy doesn't have a buck in him. I've seen him ridden for years, and he's good as gold." Mr. Davidsen huffed, slightly offended by Theresa's suggestion that his boy was anything less than perfect.

Gotcha! I'm guessing "bucks like a mad fiend" doesn't sell a horse very well, does it, Mr. Davidsen.

Marquise went home with me that day, and six months later I was still learning to trust my new partner. Trail rides with Maria and Theresa seldom encompassed more than long walks in the woods. I hadn't been ready to start trotting or cantering, but that was getting old for them, me, and especially Marquise.

With the fall fast approaching, my perfect season to begin training for a spring entrance into endurance riding arrived. No one's ever completed a race within the time limit by walking, so I had to slip on my big-girl britches.

As long as we were on the trail, my redhead was a dream, but put him in the arena, and everything changed. Once a show horse, Marquise hated mundane exercises like circling, lateral work, and collection.

I also found out Marquise didn't like canters to the left—or to the right. For that matter I'm not sure the direction had anything to do with it. He bucked every time I asked him to pick up a canter and, occasionally, in the middle of it. If the sky was blue or the grass was green, I was really in trouble. That boy of mine sure could kick up his heels.

Ride after ride, I worked on my skills, which included the watch for the lift, the emergency dismount, and the fall-softly-and-roll maneuver. I'm pleased to say we both improved. I learned to ride better and pull Marquise out of a temper tantrum, and he learned how to avoid me and get away with it if he could.

Our partnership bloomed and so did my confidence. Marquise and I began to trust each other, and with each challenge he dealt me, my survival instincts grew stronger.

"Watch it! Watch it! Watch it!" Maria screamed as a flash of gold mane ducked under my hands, and the slack in the reins disappeared. Too late. My seat lifted higher and higher, left the saddle, and floated through the air.

Marquise had pulled one of his tricks and caught me off guard.

I hit the ground heavily without an ounce of grace and rolled over to spit sand from my teeth.

"Are you okay?" Maria jogged over to check on me. She'd left Sable to wander over to Marquise, who had parked himself on the far side of the arena with his reins dragging the ground.

"I'm fine but so over this," I said, regaining my feet. I marched over to Marquise, snatched his reins from the ground, and stomped through the sand toward the gate.

"Are you going to get back on?"

I shouldn't have, but I gave my friend one of *those* looks.

"Okay, fine. I was done too."

I tied Marquise to the hitching post and pointed a finger in his direction. "You'd better think about what you've done. You...you...Ugh!" I was disgusted with my horse, but he was much more interested in his hay bag than making amends. *This is just ridiculous.* I fumed while slamming his saddle onto its rack. *Why am I tolerating this behavior when there are plenty of good horses out there that like and want to be ridden?*

My emotional train wreck worsened when I walked through the door of the house and my chipper husband met me with a smile. "Dinner's almost ready. How was your ride?"

And there went the look again.

"Geez. Sorry. It didn't go well?"

"No, it didn't." I slammed the door behind me. "I hit the dirt *again.* I'm so stinkin' sick of this. Everything is going great, and then—BAM— he goes crazy. Like seriously *Pet Cemetery* nuts. I can't figure him out, and the spring endurance season's only a couple of months away. All the girls are getting their horses ready, and I'm still figuring out how to stay on mine."

"You could sell him."

"What?" The look. "What did you say?"

"No one says you have to keep doing this. Just sell him and buy a more mellow horse. Maybe an older one with more experience would be easier for you."

Oh, no way! I wasn't going to be beaten, and I sure wasn't going to get an old horse that was more mellow and easier to ride. This battle had only just begun.

Poor God. How many times does He patiently and lovingly guide us just to have us throw Him off because we want to do our own thing and choose our own pace?

The day he chose to show his attitude, Marquise tossed me and ran to the farthest side of the arena. Can you picture how many times we must do this to God? We toss Him aside and run off. Still He patiently waits and never gives a second thought to quitting on us.

God doesn't get rid of us because of the trouble we give Him. Instead He chooses to love us more—just as I loved Marquise more and never turned my back on him. Through the trials I've had with Marquise, I've gained a new ability to ride a buck, but more importantly I've learned to appreciate the One who has never given up on me.

> No, in all these things we are more than conquerors through him who loved us. For I am convinced that neither death nor life, neither angels nor demons, neither the present nor the future, nor any powers, neither height nor depth, nor anything else in all creation, will be able to separate us from the love of God that is in Christ Jesus our Lord.
>
> Romans 8:37-39

3

Voices

Come on, Amber. You can do this.

No, I can't. I'm scared.

It's now or never. That horse is going to waste away in the pasture if you don't get on and ride.

But he bucks and will send me flying in no time.

You're a big girl. You can do this.

No, I can't.

This dialogue played in my head more times than I care to admit, and both voices shamed me.

Marquise came home with me three years earlier, and most people would've been leaving tracks on the trail by now. Not me. Nope. After my multitude of unplanned dismounts from Marquise, the thought of riding out alone still left me queasy.

My first year with Marquise was spent at a boarding barn with plenty of friends. We rode trails together, played in the arena, and camped at endurance rides. We called our campsite "Little Chicago." Pop-up canopies tied together with bungees, a camp shower partitioned with tarps, two generators, and at least three strands of Christmas lights made our campsite easy to spot and a fun home-away-from-home for a great girls' weekend.

During our second year, Marquise lived in a stall at another boarding barn. He'd torn his check ligament the previous fall at an endurance ride, and the vet advised R & R to give Marquise time to heal and hopefully get us back on the trail by the next season. After months of rehab, I moved him to my friend Erin's house for full-time turnout.

Marquise's new home sat on seven beautiful fenced acres, complete with two other horses—the things we do for those we love. Now I was alone. I'd always been at barns with lots of people around, but out there the quiet was therapeutic yet piercing.

Erin's schedule clashed with mine. We seldom saw each other and almost never found an opportunity to ride together. Time in the saddle was limited by my ability to find someone who could meet me at the trails, and that was getting old.

I decided fear would no longer control my childhood dreams, and the creak of metal as I lowered the hitch down over the tow ball seemed to approve my decision. No one else packed a saddle and hopped into the truck beside me, and no one waited for me at the trailhead. I was going alone.

Marquise, the voices, and I set out down the drive together in my gray diesel. The automatic windows slid down with a quiet hum. I tasted the flowery, spring air and tried to drown the voices *not* coming from the radio.

Oh, sister, now you're asking for it. You haven't taken this horse out alone in three years, and you think he's going to trust you just like that?

We'll be fine. I'm taking it easy.

Ha! Easy was when he launched you in the arena that day with Maria. You were taking it easy that day too.

That was then, this is now. We're much better. He trusts me more now.

Girl, it ain't got nothing to do with trust. He's a horse—you're a person. You can't reason with that.

I'll be fine! Just shut up!

I gave the volume knob on the radio a quick flick, and it roared, drowning out the battle in my head. The words of a song took life and filled the cab of my truck. Lyrics by Casting Crowns reminded me that the only voice I needed to hear was the one telling me not to be afraid, and even though what I was facing seemed more than I could bear, I had to choose to trust.

As the barn disappeared from my rearview mirror, the words swept over me and brought me a new peace. No longer did my fear and the voices control me. Peace arrived with the wave of love I felt when I realized God meant for me to hear that song just at that very moment. It was true. I had to believe, lean on His strength to overcome my fear, and trust that His comfort was always with me.

Fear doesn't just apply to horseback riding. It touches every part of our lives, from career to family, and keeps us from reaching our full potential. When we're afraid, we naturally pull away and hide behind self-made security, and when we do that, we're also pulling away from the comfort God longs to pour into us.

He doesn't want us, the children of God, to live in fear but rather to enjoy freedom that comes from knowing Him. Why then do we hesitate to trust Him? Do we not give our fears over to Christ because we think we're able to control our lives and solve our problems better than He can? If we were able to do that, why would we ever be scared to begin with?

Allowing God's Spirit to comfort and guide us requires that we let go of our fear and trust our lives into the care of His love.

> For God has not given us a spirit of fear and timidity, but of power, love, and self-discipline.
>
> **2 Timothy 1:7** NLT

4

One Deranged Goat

Hard work *does* pay off. After saving for years, Jeff and I finally purchased our dream home—a delightful five-acre farm in the country. Since he's a fantastic landscaper, Jeff had always wanted a big yard, and I welcomed the opportunity to have Marquise greet me at the gate every day. The previous owner, also a horse lover, designed it open-gate-insert-horse simple.

I thought removing Marquise from his herd and putting him into his new pasture all alone would be traumatizing, but not for my big boy. As long as grazing was plentiful, he seldom raised his nose from the ground long enough to notice if another horse was even around.

Not long after settling into our new home, I had a rare free minute at work and stole a quick peek at my e-mail in-box. Waiting for me there was a warning message—a joke that a lighthearted friend had forwarded to me about the pitfalls of animal accumulation on a farm. I giggled at the warning. It cautioned that I would soon be the owner of an old horse, a young horse, a green horse, a retired horse, a barn full of cats, a vast assortment of dogs, and at least one deranged goat.

Yeah right. I was in the country, but the country wasn't in me. There would be *no* goats in my barn.

Winter gave way to spring, and we all settled into a very simple routine. Jeff carefully tended the yard with fertilizers and crabgrass preventers, and each evening I tucked Marquise into his stall with a good-night kiss on the nose, warm mash, and fresh hay. Life was good, or so I thought.

I didn't know that I was about to be the victim of a slow, silent attack called "Empty Stall Syndrome." It's a disorder that manifests itself when a farm owner becomes aware that there are more stalls than animals. Once filling those stalls begins, it can only be stopped by reaching the end of one's bank account. The illness struck me when I least expected it. I looked around the farm and realized our numbers were multiplying and the barn and pasture sure looked like they could support another horse.

From my kitchen window, I watched Marquise carefully and began to convince myself that anytime he glanced over the fence at the neighbor's horses, his heart yearned to be with them. Contentedly swishing the flies from each other's faces and grooming itchy spots, they exuded happiness while my beloved friend stood alone.

That was it. I was a bad mother.

Once again I had to convince my animal-loving husband that we needed another one. Poor friendless Marquise just had to have a companion. Wouldn't it be terrible if Marquise became mentally unstable because of loneliness? Any truly loving husband would never knowingly allow his wife to ride a *mentally unstable* horse, would he? I finally got the answer I wanted, but he was firm on one criterion—no more horses.

On a quest I began my search for alternative livestock—cows stank, llamas bit, and sheep needed shearing. What about goats? I couldn't believe it, but a goat it would be. Now I needed to decide what kind and how many.

If you've ever searched the Internet for goats, you'll have run across some of the cutest pictures in the world. Their rabbit-like noses and cloven hooves made me want to scoop each one up onto my lap. Of course all the pictures were of the babies, but it didn't matter to me. I was sold.

In a conversation with my vet, we discussed the pros and cons of each breed of goat. *Really? Am I really having this conversation?* Luckily for me my vet raised milk goats, and two of her baby boys were weaned and looking for homes. Super excited about growing our barn family, Jeff and I hooked up the horse trailer to go pick up our new kids. We must have looked absolutely ridiculous trying to herd the little guys into the trailer. Between the two of them, they probably weighed about twenty pounds and would have easily been small enough to sit on my lap in the front seat.

Once again the family-pet-namer had a job.

"I've picked out names for the boys already," Jeff proudly said to me on the way home.

"Oh good. What are they?"

"Arn and Ole."

"Huh?"

"You know, the Anderson brothers, NWA wrestlers from the late

eighties. We won't know which will be which until we h
few days and learn their personalities. Until then we'll jus.
them 'Black Goat' and 'White Goat.'" Jeff beamed with pride. I was c
pletely speechless.

No, I didn't know the Anderson brothers, but what could I say? We
were seriously going to have baby goats named after professional wrestlers.
I bit my tongue and kept quiet. After all, Jeff hadn't insisted that I name
Marquise "Huckleberry."

Educating me on the Anderson brothers, Jeff told me the story about
how the two were a part of the wrestling group known as the "Four Horse-
men." When not performing, Ole was known to be quiet, laid-back, and
content. Arn was more of a handful, strong-willed and temperamental.
After a couple of days, Black Goat became Ole, and White Goat earned
his stripes as Arn.

Marquise immediately deemed himself caretaker and friend. He only
allowed the dogs to approach with permission, and even then he watched
them with a cautious eye. The three ate together, slept together, and on
warm days Marquise and Ole would stretch out in the sunshine barely
inches from each other while Arn remained alert as the proud herd sentinel.

Days gave way to weeks and weeks into years as the boys grew into
men. The fuzzy bundles of spindly legs and quiet bleats now tipped the
scales at two hundred and fifty pounds each. However, Ole never lived
up to the fierceness of his namesake. He remained as loving and sweet as
the day we brought him home. Always by my side at feeding time, Black
Goat was content with any kind gesture sent his way.

Oh, Arn—now that's a goat of a different color. Heaven forbid I
attempt any sort of farm-maintenance project with him around. With
the skill of a New York pickpocket, he once stole my hammer and scattered nails in a ten-foot radius before I could get the words "You stupid
goat!" out of my mouth.

On another unfortunate occasion, Arn exhibited the decorum of a
Victorian lady and the agility of a jungle cat while I was cleaning the water
trough. He felt that he just had to have one little taste of Clorox. I never
suspected a thing until it was too late. More intelligent than I ever imagined or wanted, Arn quickly learned how to pick a lock, climb a fence, and
jump out of a stall window. Unfortunately his curiosity and intelligence
didn't do him any good one fateful summer day.

Hot and sticky, the July air suffocated me as rivers of sweat ran down my brow. With a final grunt, I heaved the last bale of hay onto a stack that reached the ceiling of my extra stall. Immeasurably grateful to finally be done with the daunting task, I admired my carefully organized bales and the special alfalfa I'd tucked away in the corner. The blazing sun beat down on my now red neck. With a pompous flick, I shook the hay from my leather gloves. I was ready for winter.

The next day at work was a long one, and I desperately needed to unwind with some quiet time while feeding my special barn family. This routine was essential to my mental health.

Marquise happily met me at the fence with a noise that was part nicker and part delighted squeal, and Ole's lovable bleat warmed my heart with its long, drawn out "Maaaahm." I breathed in the peace of the moment and listened for the sound of a spastic Volkswagen Bug to shatter the serenity. The sound only a mother could love, Arn's voice always made me smile. Calling loudly, he would run toward me with those floppy ears dancing crazily on the sides of his head.

I waited a few seconds more, but the funny car horn never honked, and Arn's big ears were nowhere to be seen. I feared I was about to be searching the neighborhood for my Houdini.

God, please don't let him be on top of someone's car.

Content with their dinners, Marquise and Ole never looked up when I left them to find my trouble child. Not even ten steps later, I heard the faint cry of a very sad, lonely Volkswagen. The pitiful sound led me to the stall sheltering my cherished winter hay, and I gasped at the sight before me.

Arn had climbed the gate that guarded my treasure of soft, succulent hay, scaled the neatly stacked bales, collapsed the stacks, and proceeded to gorge himself.

Ten... nine... eight... seven... six... five... four... three... two... one. I counted down slowly and measured the distance between him and me by the mountain of twenty or so hay bales separating us. This would be no easy rescue, so I gathered what little patience remained and grabbed the top of the gate.

After hauling myself over and dropping into the elaborate disaster beneath me, I took a good look at the little menace. Standing sheepishly among some very fine looking alfalfa, his swollen belly told the tale of what he'd been doing all day.

Half an hour later, I was sweating profusely and covered from head to toe with the itchy forage, but my child was safe. Hindered by his waistline, Arn awkwardly waddled over to his friends. Rather than shoving his nose into their bowls and looking for any left-over morsels, the glutton laid down on his favorite patch of grass. Clearly my white goat was feeling quite green.

On more than one occasion, I've done the exact same thing. I saw something that looked like a great idea, forged ahead, and ended up in a tough situation.

I've tried to fix these things myself but have learned from experience that I can't do it alone. God tells us to trust Him no matter what situation we are in. His ways are not our ways. By trying to take control, we can ruin our day.

Our future is always filled with uncertainty, and it can be tempting to take matters into our own hands and make decisions based on what we think is right. Whether money, career, or family—whatever is weighing you down—put it before the Lord. Ask Him what His plan is before you make a decision that locks you in and turns you green.

> Trust in the LORD with all your heart and do not lean on your own understanding. In all your ways acknowledge Him, and He will make your paths straight.
>
> **Proverbs 3:5-6** NASB

5

Fit to Continue

"To finish is to win." The motto of the American Endurance Ride Conference emphasizes the health of a horse through the entirety of an endurance ride—regardless of how it places. Solitary riding, fatigue, and mental stress combine in a grueling test of perseverance that can't be won by fitness alone. One must also have a fierce will.

Even so, the race doesn't end at the finish line. A completion will be awarded only after a vet carefully examines a horse's hydration, movement, attitude, and gut sounds and determines if it's healthy enough to go back out on the trail. Many never make it to this point. Hazardous conditions, rugged terrain, unpredictable weather, and other horses can all hinder a horse-and-rider team's progress. Only the most fit will endure the miles.

After our first race, my stomach churned while I waited to present Marquise for his completion exam. I'd ridden carefully but was still learning the ins and outs of the sport. It wouldn't be unheard of for a newbie to ride too fast, too hard, or make one of many other possible mistakes.

Mentally and physically exhausted, I ran my hand over the long tight tendons of Marquise's wet legs and searched for heat or pain. Finding none I turned my attention to his bright eyes that reflected the summer sun. He scanned the ocean of horses surrounding us and called for his bay buddy who'd camped beside him for the last couple of days. Marquise seemed alert enough, and his occasional tug on the halter was still strong. He wanted to go back out, but that wasn't my call, and my doubts had me second-guessing the decisions I'd made through the day.

Had I chosen the right electrolytes, stopped enough to let him drink, and kept a safe pace that was right for him? Marquise's strength increased so much through the day that we cantered the whole last loop. Was that wrong? Was I asking him for something I wanted rather than what was best for him?

"Next rider, please!" The irritated voice snapped me back to reality.

While lost in my thoughts, my turn had come. My eyes immediately locked with those of the vet staring at Marquise and me. Not waiting for us to reach him, the vet's discerning eyes immediately went to work and dissected Marquise's every move. My heart thumped as we walked the twenty or so feet toward our judgment.

Asking about the decisions I'd made during the day, the vet wanted nothing less than a completely honest account. My time of judgment had come. Would I be able to finish the race?

"How does he feel?" The vet was talking to me, but his eyes didn't leave the equine in front of him. He ran his hands along Marquise's neck, back, and legs.

"He's been good and strong all day. It's our first competition, so, of course, I'm a little concerned about how well he's fared." I answered truthfully but wasn't sure if he heard my response. He'd already plugged his ears with the hard, plastic tips of a stethoscope and moved it around my horse's belly, strategically listening for gut sounds.

"He cantered strong for almost that whole last loop. We were having so much fun riding around the big lake, and then we came up on some day riders…" My voice trailed off when I got the look and raised eyebrows from the vet. He was holding his stethoscope behind Marquise's left elbow and was patiently waiting for me to end my chatter long enough for him to hear the rhythmical lub-dub of Marquise's heart.

He removed the stethoscope from his ears and looped it over the collar of his thin plaid button-up. "Trot please."

We did. Marquise pulled me along with his head high and a longer stride than what we'd practiced at home. At the cone forty meters out, we turned around, and I snagged another breath that I hoped would be enough to get me back to the vet. Dry dust kicked up at Marquise's back hooves as he dug in to stop. I suppressed my need to bend over and grab my knees to catch my breath, but instead gritted my teeth, smiled, and made a mental note to start jogging.

"He was a bit much on that trot out. You should probably keep working on that at home," said the man in the plaid shirt before sticking the plastic and metal back into his ears to count out Marquise's cardiac recovery. I held my breath and waited. "He's good—50/48," he reported to the scribe who scribbled the heart rate numbers on my vet card and handed it back to me. "Looks like you could go back out if you wanted." This time the vet finally looked directly at me and smiled. Passing my first vet check with my horse was a personal victory.

Our spiritual race is run against the sin of this world. To withstand it, we must be prepared. To build our spiritual strength and endurance, we can rely on many things: time spent in prayer and in the Word, fellowship with other believers, and reliance on the leadership and lordship of Christ. If we put these things to use, we will prevail.

We're all going to face a time when, rather than presenting a strong horse to the vet for his examination, we're going to be presenting ourselves to God. He will question if we lived for Him unselfishly and for His glory or if we sought our own happiness and personal gain.

Although our salvation is secure through Christ alone, we will still have to answer whether or not our actions in this life honored the kingdom that awaits us. When we, as followers of Christ, proudly stand before Him and give an honest account of our salvation and personal relationship with Jesus Christ, we will be deemed fit to continue into an eternal life with Him in paradise.

> I have fought the good fight, I have finished the race, I have kept the faith. Now there is in store for me the crown of righteousness, which the Lord, the righteous Judge, will award to me on that day—and not only to me, but also to all who have longed for his appearing.
>
> 2 Timothy 4:7-8

6

That Kind of Friend

Endurance had gotten under my skin, and I loved it. Nickers of horses in the early morning hours, long talks with fellow riders, cold nights spent in leaky tents, and pain the morning after a good ride—it was all addictive. My friends and I made it to as many rides as we could, and even if we couldn't ride together, we made sure to at least be there to support and crew for the other one.

Theresa had been training a young horse named Harley and building up his competition mileage when acute appendicitis struck. She was out for her next race, but being the friend I was, I stepped up and offered to take her place in the saddle.

I spent the following weeks getting familiar with Harley, talking strategy with Theresa, and making camp preparations. We agreed my goal should simply be to cross the finish line—on top of the horse.

With the foresight of a seasoned competitor, Theresa knew that on ride morning Harley could quickly pull a Jekyll and Hyde. Hoping to avoid this, Theresa arranged for me to ride with Maria, a good friend of hers, and a group of girls who planned just to have fun.

I'd never met Maria and was anxious about tackling my first ride on a new horse with a group of complete strangers. How was I going to tack up, get Harley warm and ready, and make it to the starting line on time—much less attempt to be social?

The early October morning dawned crisp and cool, and my nerves made sure I was awake in time to get everything done. After a final tack check and cheerful words of encouragement, Theresa gave me a leg up. My seat touched the saddle, and I met Mr. Hyde.

Harley was fit, inexperienced, and ready to run with the herd. Even the best preparation couldn't have braced me for the shock. He jigged and pranced while whipping his tail ferociously from side to side and calling to the hundred or so other horses doing the same. My chest tightened, and I swallowed hard against the lump in my throat. Things got worse when the trail opened up and the chaotic mass of horses raced ahead into the cloud of early morning fog. I never saw Maria and the girls who waited for me.

The behemoth beneath me fought for his head with surprising strength as I struggled to maintain some sort of control. In an act of desperation, I made a terrible decision and released my hold on the reins to let Harley go.

The situation between me and the now raging fury didn't improve as we raced down the trail. The trees flew by as I gave way to panic. With amazing velocity a series of ill-fated events led to moments of sheer terror, and I ended up hanging crazily off the angry horse's side.

After a hopeless effort to delay the inevitable, I crashed against the ground. A painful cry escaped my lips as Harley's merciless hooves pounded my frame before he disappeared in pursuit of the herd.

If only I'd waited for Maria.

A couple of days after the accident, Maria called. Surely she planned to chide me for my poor decision, but with the stitches still fresh and my body still aching, I was hardly in the mood to be reprimanded by a stranger.

Several days passed, and she tried to contact me again. This time she stopped by my office and dropped off a sweet note with her phone number. Defeated, I made up my mind to get the "You should have…" speech over with.

A few short minutes into the conversation, it became apparent Maria truly cared about me and wasn't interested in pointing fingers. She not only wanted to know how I was healing physically, but she also recognized the scars of fear. We talked regularly and when the time was right, she gently encouraged me to ride her horse, Sable. I was still healing, but Maria knew the best way for me to be whole again was to get back in the saddle.

After avoiding the issue for a while, I finally made myself go to the barn with her. As I cautiously approached Sable, the same fear from that cool October morning crept in. I ran my trembling fingers through his blood-bay coat and gazed deep into his coal-black eyes that assured me that soon all would be well again. As a patient teacher, he promised to remind me how to be bold, but as an Arabian, he wouldn't guarantee it'd be easy.

Maria and I spent many hours simply walking our horses around the pasture. Maria rode Marquise while I rode Sable, who was always eager to help build my confidence. Once I felt bold enough to graduate from quiet walks, I put on my big-girl britches and attempted my first trot. My new friend encouraged these baby steps and was there the whole time, tirelessly supporting me and pushing me when I needed it.

Typical of a strong-willed Arabian, Sable sometimes felt the need to express his opinion about this annoyingly simple, drawn-out schooling. He was accustomed to clicking off the miles like a race car at Daytona. Built for speed and endurance, babysitting me wasn't his idea of a good time.

The day he'd finally had enough, Sable defiantly dropped his transmission into park. Clearly we weren't going anywhere without a fight. Stinging tears immediately blurred my vision, and the burn of adrenaline rushed through my body. I wanted to quit. Confident her horse was all bark and no bite, Maria wasn't about to let that happen.

The next few minutes defined the rest of my life with horses.

"Can I get off for a few minutes?" My eyebrows crinkled in the middle with the worried question.

"No. You're fine. Stick with him." Maria knew this was one of those times she needed to push me rather than ease off.

"But—" Arguing wouldn't do me any good at this point. Sable had already left the arena and taken me with him. He wasn't out of control. He was in control, and I wasn't.

"Don't let him do that. He's taking advantage of you, and you're letting him."

"He's not listening."

"He's not listening because you aren't making him. Sit deep, drop your heels, and make him get away from that gate."

I'd let Sable take us all the way out of the arena and over to the pasture gate. He stood with his head hanging over it and waited on a passerby to open it. I tried the reins but got a rebellious shake of the head. I squeezed his sides with my legs and nearly panicked when I felt his haunches lower and his front end lighten.

"Do not let him get away with that!" Maria's voice was firmer than I'd heard before. Even though I wanted to bail, I knew there was no way she was would let me, so I dug in.

Maria patiently worked with Sable and me and brought us back into harmony as horse and rider. When my feet touched the ground that day, I was emotionally drained but had found renewed confidence. My demons of fear had attacked, and with the help of my new friend, I had won.

The Bible tells the story of a great friendship between David and Jonathan. God placed these two young men in each other's lives to be an example to us of the love of a true friend. Jonathan loved David as himself. As the son of the king, Jonathan was distraught when he learned of his father's extreme jealousy and secret plan to murder David. Despite knowing he would be killed for this act of treason, Jonathan devised a plan to help his friend flee unharmed. Jonathan's selfless love for David ran deep and was the motivation that fueled his actions to the point that he was willing to give up his own life for his friend's.

Are you *that* kind of friend? Can your friends count on you through the good times and the bad, or are you only available when it's convenient? Sometimes loving someone is difficult. It often means we must set our wants and desires aside, but when we act selflessly and put another's needs before our own, we are in a position to be *that* kind of friend.

Two are better than one, because they have a good return for their labor: If either of them falls down, one can help the other up. But pity anyone who falls and has no one to help them up. Also, if two lie down together, they will keep warm. But how can one keep warm alone? Though one may be overpowered, two can defend themselves. A cord of three strands is not quickly broken.

Ecclesiastes 4:9-12

7

Experience—the Better Teacher?

If you have a horse, there's a better than average chance you also own a dog. Maybe it's a purebred wiry thing that finds its way into your saddle-bag or the front seat of your truck. Perhaps it's an oversized leggy one with floppy ears that looks out of place in the house, but in the pasture with the ponies, it looks right at home. More than likely, it's just a dawg. Brown, white, black, or spotted, it doesn't matter. They all give us their hearts and steal ours.

Over the years Jeff and I have adopted two dogs, a large female and a small male. Four years apart in age, they look like they came from the same lab and Heinz 57 litter. Although they're almost identical in physical appearance, their personalities are as different as night and day. The older one, Hootie, is smart, athletic, independent, and not overly affectionate. Tully is the polar opposite. Small and sweet, his favorite pastime is lying in your lap begging for a belly scratch.

Before Tully, Hootie lived the life of a queen. She ate, slept, and offered careful supervision of my evening barn chores. Life was good. Little did she know, my friend Kelly was about to change her world forever.

Kelly had found what she thought would be a great addition to our family. He was being fostered by a rescue group, but in only a few days, he'd be sent to the local shelter. Jeff loves animals as much as I do, so we quickly came to the rescue.

An engraved collar and open arms were waiting for Tully when he arrived. He wanted nothing more than to give us his love, but he was too weak from neglect to even climb up on the couch to cuddle with us.

Somehow Hootie, normally a jealous only child, knew Tully needed a family. Unlike times when other dogs have come over to play or be a house guest for the weekend, Hootie welcomed Tully easily, and the two immediately became fast friends.

Every day the two tumble in the yard until their heads, tails, legs, and ears morph into a singular ball of fur. Somehow in these wrestling matches, Tully always reigns as the victor. Hootie knows he's small and nonthreatening, so she lets the diminutive guy feel powerful. If Hootie ever stops for a breather, she's immediately bombarded with barking and ear biting, which provokes a second wind, and they go at it again.

Tully's second choice for a playmate is Marquise. Outweighed by half a ton, Tully has no clue that the odds are stacked heavily against him and fearlessly barks for attention. Marquise maintains his composure as long as Tully stays on the other side of the fence and only occasionally flicks an ear in the direction of the yapping irritant. Tully would love nothing more than to get into the pasture for some real fun, but the normally mild-mannered Marquise can become very cranky when he's annoyed.

⬥

One winter night we were outside with friends stacking wood for a bonfire in our top pasture. We needed to leave the gate to the road open, so without thinking I locked the dogs in the lower field with Marquise and the goats.

Not long into our work, we heard the telltale bark of a little dog wanting to play. The nagging stopped as quickly as it started, so we continued planning our inferno. Sweaty and cold we finished our work and closed the gate to let the dogs join us.

Tully wagged his whole body as he introduced himself to our guests and made sure they had been sufficiently kissed and sniffed. When the welcome rounds were complete, he stopped in front of Jeff who noticed a small trickle of blood running down the pup's cheek. The dark made it hard to see the damage, but Tully's happy tail assured us he hadn't been slowed down a bit.

Tully was the victim of a warning kick.

Horses have two speeds of kicks. The first is the warning kick. It's the one that lets you know whatever you're doing is not appreciated. The second is the "You're going to land in the next county" kick. Tully had received the former and retreated before receiving the latter. I had warned and scolded Tully, but this time experience was the better teacher.

Why is that? Why does it take learning the hard way to show us that what we do—or don't do—can yield painful consequences for ourselves or others? Why can't we just listen to the wise counsel that surrounds us and offers to help us stay out of bad situations?

Wise counsel can come in many forms. It can come as advice from a friend, spouse, coworker, or family member. No matter who we choose to turn to, the counsel we seek should always be based on the Word of God. When listening to advice and trying to sort out a decision, falling into the trap of heeding the world's advice is easy. Be wary of this because often what appears right can be perfectly in line with today's culture but completely against God's will.

Tully chose to let experience be his teacher, but listening to wise counsel would have saved him the headache.

> The fear of the LORD is the beginning of knowledge: but fools despise wisdom and instruction.
>
> **Proverbs 1:7** KJV

8

DeBerry Best

Throughout a lifetime, a horse lover will own several horses and have many friends who will do the same. Some horses will do only what is asked of them, and some will reach deeper and touch the very essence of who we are. I call these "soul-mate horses." My friend Theresa was privileged enough to be chosen by her soul-mate horse.

Seyvilla DeBerry was a picture of majesty. His fine Arabian features seemed to be carved from precious gems, and his mane floated in the air like threads of spun silk. Deep muscles rippled under his auburn coat, and when he moved, his strong legs devoured the earth beneath him. The bond between horse and rider captivated anyone who witnessed their shared love for a long breathless gallop.

As in any relationship, these two had their moments. I was crewing for them at an endurance ride when they stormed into the vet-check area obviously in the middle of a bitter disagreement. In true Arabian style, DeBerry made the argument look like art. His chestnut tail flagged back and forth against his glistening body as his nostrils flared with impatience. Pounding the earth, he defiantly circled Theresa in disapproval.

Red-faced, winded, and more resolute than ever, Theresa held fast to the reins with her bloody fingers. "I can be way more stubborn and for way longer than you *ever* dreamed possible!" she said. "Just give up now, and we'll both be much happier."

Relying on firmness and determination, Theresa always had a way of leading her horses through their differences. Negotiating many of these difficult miles together strengthened their relationship, and in time a partnership of great love and respect was born.

On March 13, 2008, Theresa and the girls pulled into the Sandhills Endurance Ride campsite. It was a beautiful Thursday night, and they had arrived early to make Friday a day of rest before the race on Saturday. After setting up camp and enjoying a quick dinner, everyone wearily retired to their respective cots, sleeping bags, and horse trailers. The quiet of the night crept in, enveloping riders and horses alike.

Typical for Theresa, she woke up in the wee hours of the morning to savor the quiet and check on DeBerry.

The comforting peace faded the second she stepped out of her trailer. All wasn't well with the world. Fear seized her when she discovered DeBerry and his buddy Sammy were both missing from their corral. The breath ripped from her lungs as she ran toward the sound of painful groans.

Theresa's beloved partner lay on the ground writhing in pain, and Sammy stood by DeBerry's side. With sad knowing eyes, he kept quiet vigil over his friend. Strangulation colic, resulting from a prior tumor removal, had begun quickly and rapidly progressed to a critical stage. Theresa called the vet immediately, but her fear of the near future loomed.

Theresa never left the side of her precious companion. Rubbing his velvet muzzle and stroking his neck, she tenderly whispered prayers and begged him not to leave her. Through the burn of her unrelenting tears, she looked straight into his soul. His heart, which had given her unconditional love, was failing.

At this race she knew they wouldn't cross the finish line together. Heartache shook Theresa to her very core. As he took his last breath, she whispered a final farewell to Seyvilla DeBerry, and he crossed his final finish line—alone.

Life is full of sorrow, hurt, and loss. It's during these times that we want to know why. Is God mad at us? Does He not love us anymore? How can such a good God let bad things happen to us, His children?

The truth is this: God never leaves us alone when we're suffering. In fact He promises He'll never let anything come our way that we haven't been prepared to face.

Job was a holy man, favored by God. For this Satan sought to destroy

Job and asked God's permission to test him. Satan's desire was to take Job's health, wealth, and family in such painful ways that Job would curse God and turn from Him. However, God knew His servant was faithful, and through these trials Job's faith would grow stronger. That's why God allowed the evil.

Job lost all his riches, his family, and his health. Even then he praised the name of the Lord by saying, "Naked I came from my mother's womb, and naked I will depart. The LORD gave and the LORD has taken away; may the name of the LORD be praised" (Job 1:21). Job knew that no matter what happened to him or his family and though the certainty of his future was lost, the greater power of God was at work. It was all part of a much bigger plan, and through his trials and faithfulness, Job was restored and remained a devoted servant of the Lord.

When we face trials and pain, God draws near to us and offers His outstretched arms of comfort. His strength allows us to emerge from the darkest valleys stronger and more resolute in our faith.

We as horse lovers are blessed to be able to love an animal that can honestly and completely love us back. God touches us through them, and even when the last breath is gone and the last gallop has been run, His arms remain.

> The LORD is my shepherd; I shall not want.
>
> He maketh me to lie down in green pastures: he leadeth me beside the still waters.
>
> He restoreth my soul: he leadeth me in the paths of righteousness for his name's sake.
>
> Yea, though I walk through the valley of the shadow of death, I will fear no evil: for thou art with me; thy rod and thy staff they comfort me.
>
> Thou preparest a table before me in the presence of my enemies: thou anointest my head with oil; my cup runneth over.
>
> Surely goodness and mercy shall follow me all the days of my life: and I will dwell in the house of the LORD for ever.

Psalm 23 KJV

9

The Endurance Bible

My eyes locked on the sight in front of me as the commotion from the endurance camp faded into background noise. Towering overhead were sixty feet of aluminum and steel. The decked-out trailer glinted in the sun like the tail of a midnight comet. From the arms of its awning, multi-colored T-shirts and tights hung from a makeshift clothesline. Beneath the assortment of clothing, rope-handled muck buckets marked "clearance" dotted the outdoor carpet's black and tan horse pattern. That day I learned that it's common for vendors to show up at the larger endurance rides with fully stocked big rigs like an equestrian Walmart on wheels.

A used trail saddle with a handwritten "For Sale" sign rested on a wooden rack. The rubs on its seat told tales of countless adventures, and if it could talk, the sweet-smelling leather would reveal secrets shared only between horse and rider. More tempting than the splendor before me was the simple word on the mat placed casually in front of the rig's open door—Welcome. It beckoned me to step into the rabbit hole and enter Wonderland. I feared that if I stepped too close, I would break the spell, and the magic would be gone. So I just stood there gawking.

"Are you going in or not?"

I whipped my head toward the voice only to see the figure sweep around me, step over the welcome mat, and disappear into the darkened doorway.

It was real.

This was my big break. I'd been reading everything I could get my hands on about endurance riding and was finally ready to quit playing and get serious. I decided that day was the beginning of *my* time. It was

time for me to break into the big league, make my mark, and learn *all* of
the hidden endurance secrets. It was time for me to have my own copy of
The Endurance Bible.

Within its sacred pages, I'd unearth writings as treasured and myste-
rious as the Dead Sea Scrolls and gain all the knowledge needed to have
a successful competitive season. With anxious anticipation, I yearned
to discover absolute truths about feeding, conditioning, tack, electrolytes, hoof care, ride strategy, and more. So with cash in hand, I pur-
posefully stepped through the door of the trailer and disappeared into
Wonderland.

My heart skipped a beat as my eyes danced over the brilliant colors that
lined the walls and hung from the ceiling. A rainbow of BioThane tack
loudly boasted every color imaginable. With my mouth watering worse
than Pavlov's dog, I counted my money and compared the meager amount
in my hand to the price tags dangling from the vendor's merchandise.

Wistfully I imagined Marquise flying down the trail in all this finery
as we pursued our renewed dedication to the sport. Everything my heart
desired for the perfect ride was right there at my fingertips. By simply
switching from cash to credit, I would be well on the way to my dream.

After a brief but intense battle between the noble angel on my right
shoulder and the naughty one on my left, I dodged temptation and
reminded myself that I was there for one reason and one reason only—
to buy *my* treasured copy of *The Endurance Bible*. Motivated by focus, I
swept some neon-colored reins to the side and peered down at a small
dusty shelf that held a paltry assortment of books.

Though the choices were limited, I was at an endurance event looking
for an endurance book, so I knew this was the right place. After a quick
thorough skim through the titles, I found books about equine massage,
arena exercises, and animal communication but came up empty-handed
in the search for my treasure. Not one given to premature panic, I assured
myself that this item was either sold out or not yet unpacked.

I boldly made my way to the front of the trailer where sales were being
rung up. When my turn came, the vendor's eyes held a question as they
fixed on my empty hands. When I explained my dilemma, her eyes started
to twinkle.

"Honey, you're looking for what?" she asked, obviously enjoying my conundrum. The corners of her lips twitched with the beginning of a smile.

"*The Endurance Bible*." I really didn't understand why this was so difficult.

"Sugar, there's no such thing. Are you new to the sport?"

Now I felt like I was being patronized by my grandmother. "No, well—yes. Not really. I'm just looking for a book with all the answers. Marquise and I have been taking some time off from competing, and we're ready to start up again. I just need to know everything so I can do things right."

I was thankful for her professionalism as she tried desperately to hide her amusement. "Darlin', if there's anything I've learned from the years I've been in this sport, it's that every horse is different, every day is different, and every trail is different. You can't always depend on the same thing to get you through today that got you through yesterday. You need to know concepts about training, weather, and nutrition, but above all, you have to know your horse."

Hope left me with a wimper, and I barely listened to the rest of her sales pitch as she led me back to the dusty shelf. Shaken and frustrated, I absentmindedly thumbed through the pages of a couple of the books, purchased one with the best cover, and walked out in a daze.

Since my defeat I've learned to rely on the knowledge of my experienced friends. Each time I ask questions about training, feeding, and ride technique, I inwardly cringe when I'm reminded that there is no *Endurance Bible,* and there never will be. Through trial and error, I'll find a winning combination and cross the finish line windblown and deeper in love with a very happy horse.

Thankfully we *do* have a book we can depend on. The Bible. The words on its pages are useful for inspiration and instruction as well as discipline. It's always right and without fault in all circumstances. Though it's not a magic book with instant answers to every question, it does direct us toward God and His will. The more we get to know Him and His character, the easier it becomes to decipher what's right and what's wrong.

When the trail of life gets confusing, all we have to do is open our Bible and relax. In its sacred words, we learn more about God, the perfect example He left, and the answers to some of our greatest mysteries.

> Such things were written in the Scriptures long ago to teach us. And the Scriptures give us hope and encouragement as we wait patiently for God's promises to be fulfilled.
>
> **Romans 15:4** NLT

10

Guardian Angels

Humidity dotted Maria's gray T-shirt with charcoal spots, making it stick to her back as she bent over the hitch of her old, steel horse trailer. A bead of sweat sped down her porcelain forehead toward her crystal blue eyes before it was rerouted down her jawline. A glance through the window at the thermometer on the truck's dashboard revealed that the temperature was ninety-five degrees—brutally hot for eleven in the morning, even in South Carolina.

After kicking the hitch into the locked position, she made her way around to each of the tires to double-check their pressure before beginning her four-hour trip. The two-horse, straight-load was nothing to look at, but it was safe, secure, and had made many memorable trips down that same southbound interstate.

The trailer tires crunched the gravel, and the empty steel rattled behind the red F-250. Maria steered down her driveway toward Statesboro, Georgia, to meet a chestnut Arabian mare named Farah. A friend of the family whose health had been plagued with illness had offered the horse to Maria as a gift, and to refuse a horse from the lineage of Witraz, Raffles, and Bask would have been obscene.

Green mile markers slipped by unnoticed until they disappeared past the corner of the windshield. Maria exited to the right and turned her attention to county road signs and small towns to navigate the last eighty miles. Pulling a trailer always slowed her down, whether it was loaded or not, and her cautious driving had increased the length of the trip. As she turned into the rutted rural driveway, she calculated a one-hour pickup would still leave plenty of sun to haul Farah home before the late summer sunset.

Signs of disrepair were evidence of the farm owner's illness. The arena—training grounds of past Scottsdale competitors—was ringed by broken boards that hung haphazardly from fence posts. Paint had peeled off in sheets and lay in small piles to crumble into dust or be carried away by the breeze. The west corner of the barn weighed heavily with a creeping tangled mass of ivy that threatened to tear away its support while needling through open windows and into rank hay bales.

Maria's damp nervous fingers slipped on her door handle as she pressured it to open, and when her boots touched the red clay, she saw an older woman and a younger man step through the doorway of the whitewashed home. The sprawling porch, the setting of bygone memories, was disgraced by maintenance needs overlooked during months of doctor's appointments.

"Hey, I'm Maria." Discreetly wiping her sweaty palm against her faded Levis, she stretched her right hand toward the two who'd just taken the last step off the slightly lopsided front porch.

"I'm so happy you're here," the woman said as she bypassed Maria's hand to lean in for an unexpected hug. "Your mother told me so much about you. I'm so happy you can take Farah for me. Since my Jim died, I just can't keep up with the place anymore. Little Jimmy, my son here, tries to help, but he's got a family, and they're just not interested in horses." The older woman's eyes welled up. Jimmy rested his arm around his mother's shoulders to ease her sadness. "Well, honey, I'm betting you'd rather meet Farah than stand here talking to an old woman. She's in the back."

When they rounded the corner of the house, Maria noticed the refined features of the young mare. Farah stood patiently at the hitching post with her thick, cotton lead rope draped loosely, not tied, to its ring. Looking docile enough, she followed Maria with her warm brown eyes and flared her nostrils to take in the scent of the unfamiliar guest.

"She seems like a sweet girl," Maria said as she stroked the shoulder of the young horse and tried to decide if she glowed more copper or bronze.

"Oh, she is. More like a pet than a horse. Jim had a trainer put sixty days on her, but that was years ago, before…" Her voice trailed off. Clearly rehoming her horses was about more than getting them off her feed bill. She was taking another step in the healing process by letting them go.

"I'll take her," Maria said. There was no way she could allow such a beautiful animal to continue keeping a heart wound open in this woman.

"Are you sure? Don't you want to ride her?"

"No. I've got a long drive ahead of me, and I'm going to have just enough time to make it home before the sun goes down. Are you sure I can't give you any money for her?"

"No, dear. Just take her and love her like my sweet Jim did. He always loved the red ones best."

"I will, and don't you worry a moment about her. She'll do just fine."

Maria has many strengths as an equestrian—quiet hands, a balanced seat, and the ability to load difficult horses into any trailer. Farah was no exception. Though she'd been in a trailer only a few times during training and never to travel, it took only ten minutes for Maria to have the horse standing quietly and munching on hay in the manger.

"Beautiful," the woman said. "Just beautiful." Without another word she turned, hobbled up the porch stairs, and disappeared into the house.

"She doesn't want to watch Farah leave," Little Jimmy said in an effort to explain his mother's odd behavior. "Do you need anything before you go?"

"No. We'll be fine. Thank you." Maria confidently latched the half door behind the young mare. "As soon as we get back to the interstate, we'll be halfway home."

"Well, good luck to you. My daddy would be proud."

"Thank you for trusting me with her." This time Maria was prepared for the awkward embrace that she graciously accepted before climbing back into the truck.

<hr />

She may have loaded easily, but Farah had never traveled, nor had she ever been out of a herd. Now she was trapped in a noisy steel box and confined on all sides—the perfect combination for disaster.

Maria could see from her rearview mirror that the copper-colored horse was no longer quiet. The green Plexiglas at the front of the trailer allowed only a shadowy view of the scene that played out behind her truck bed. Farah stomped and threw her body from side to side, jolting the trailer against the big truck and threatening to knock the whole rig off the road.

"Come on, girl. Calm down. This can't go on."

Farah's erratic behavior didn't stop by the time they met back up with the interstate, so Maria chose to take the first exit to a large truck stop. Opening the manger door allowed Farah to force her head out into the open and blow hard against the strange air.

"It's going to be okay. I promise," Maria said as she stroked the tiny strip of white that now glowed a wet pink down the middle of Farah's dished face. "Just a little farther. All we have left is interstate, and before you know it, you'll be in your new pasture." While she talked soothingly to the young horse, Maria gathered up the slack in the lead rope to keep Farah from spinning around in the trailer and getting wedged against the center divider. "You're a good girl. We'll be home soon." After adding a new flake of hay to the manger, Maria closed the door with a prayer that the next few hours would pass quickly.

Merging into the interstate traffic, Maria turned off the radio to focus all her attention on her precious new cargo. No sooner had Maria leaned back against her seat than transfer trucks began to speed past the little trailer. Their draft sucked the trailer toward the center line before pushing it away and off the road's shoulder. It quickly became too much. Farah's stomping and banging exploded as the noise ricocheted through the trailer. Horror permeated the steel coffin-on-wheels while the terrified thrashing continued—until Maria felt a heavy jerk.

In an instant all went quiet.

Maria's white knuckles clutched the wheel as she glanced away from the road and into her mirror. Farah's shadow was gone.

Panic caught in Maria's throat. In seconds gravel spun, and the truck skidded to a stop on the shoulder of I-20. Slamming the Ford into park, Maria jumped out, ran around to the back of the trailer, and leapt up on the fender to look over the rear half-doors.

The whizzing cars from the interstate didn't slow down—though Maria's world did. The smell of rubber on asphalt and the heavy drone of traffic added to the backdrop of Maria's harrowing reality. What she saw collapsed on the rubber mats of the floor was the motionless body of her delicate mare.

Farah, covered in white lathered sweat, lay on her back—eyes open yet empty and eerily still. Maria gasped as her hand shot up to cover her mouth. She scanned the body and searched for signs of life. Only the ragged rise and fall of inconsistent breaths suggested there was still hope.

Maria's thoughts began to race as she realized the extreme danger. In Farah's panic, she'd flipped over, knocked herself out cold, and now lay directly beneath the center divider. If Maria couldn't work quickly to remove the divider before the horse woke up and began struggling to regain her footing, a bad situation would become disastrous.

Leaning over the doors on the back of the trailer, Maria pulled the divider pin. It came loose, but the divider wouldn't budge. Hastily she hopped off the fender and ran to the manger door, flung it open, and wriggled her body through the small opening to pull the pin from that end as well. It was useless. The old steel was firmly in place.

Glancing down at the crumpled mass at the end of the trailer, Maria's heart froze as she watched Farah begin to wake up. Fear gave way to panic, and Maria slipped from reality. Her breath came in short gasps. Willing her legs to catch her, she jumped from the manger window and ran the few steps to the back of the trailer just in time to see a black Dodge Durango pull up.

From the driver's side, a tall leathered cowboy stepped out. He looked out of place on the South Carolina interstate, but for Maria he looked perfect. Without a moment's hesitation or request for permission, he jumped onto the back fender to glance inside.

His capable hands curled around the half-door as Farah woke and began her struggle. The sound of metal rang out as she shook her head from side to side, crashing it loudly against the trailer as she tried to right herself. Her hooves struck out as they sought footing, but they found only air. Farah's terror escalated.

With a sharp bang and a powerful thrust, Farah's hooves connected with the center divider. It was only by God's intervention that the steel shot into the air directly over the fearful horse's body and came to rest against the trailer wall just as perfectly as if it'd been set there by human hands. Clear to get up, Farah lunged upward and toward escape. Her dark eyes were filled with panic as she sought refuge.

The Durango cowboy took charge and raised his large hands in front of the half-doors, breaking up the visual appearance of freedom. No longer having to think for herself, Maria followed suit by waving her hands upward and quickly grew fearful of how long this could go on.

In the commotion Maria and the cowboy hadn't seen a red sports car pull up behind the Durango. A young woman with black hair tied back into a ponytail ran toward the trailer. "What can I do?" she shouted.

"Stand here and do what I'm doing," said the cowboy. "Whatever you do, don't let that horse get past you, or we'll have a real mess on our hands. I'm going to call a vet to sedate this crazy mare."

<hr />

Within forty-five minutes, Farah stood in the trailer with her head hanging down to her knees. A thin line of blood trickling from her nostrils was all that indicated her near-fatal accident.

"Sir, I can't thank you enough for stopping. I don't know how this would have turned out if it hadn't been for you. Why'd you stop anyway?"

"Well, there's a lot of crazy in my line of work, and I do whatever I can to help out. This isn't the first time I've seen a near disaster. Usually I just expect it at work and not while I'm mindin' my own business drivin' down the interstate."

"You see this a lot? What do you do anyway?"

"I'm a rodeo clown, ma'am."

In the midst of the conversation and Maria's musing, the red sports car that had disappeared during the vet's sedation pulled back up, and the woman with the black ponytail reappeared. "I saw that the horse broke her halter, and I knew you would need one wherever you were going. I picked this one up for you from the tack store up the road a little ways." The woman offered up a new royal blue halter and lead rope. Maria smiled as she reached for them, knowing how sharp they would look on her new girl.

"I can follow you home if you need me to. I don't know much about horses, but at least this guy taught me a thing or two about keeping them from jumping out windows."

The new group of friends smiled knowing that without each one of them, the day could have ended with a red fireball running down I-20. Likely the horse's life and others were spared because a few strangers worked together.

Until that day Maria might not have known the answer to whether or not guardian angels exist. Nevertheless, now she knows there are people who are allowed and possibly even sent by God to intercede on the behalf of others. That day on the interstate, countless people drove past Maria's trailer, and many of them would've been in the same near-panic state when they realized the situation.

Maria will always say her guardian angels came that day in the form of a Durango cowboy and willing young woman with a black ponytail. Those two people saw a need and stepped in to fill it even though they weren't asked. Sometimes a request for help doesn't come in the form of a question but more by a situation. We just have to be ready to help others when God puts that situation before us.

> Keep on loving one another as brothers and sisters. Do not forget to show hospitality to strangers, for by so doing some people have showed hospitality to angels without knowing it.
>
> **Hebrews 13:1-2**

11

Get to the Root of the Problem

"So I think Listerine is a good idea," Erin said.

"You're kidding, right?" We weren't talking about dental care, so I didn't know why Erin had mentioned it.

"I heard somewhere that Listerine could help skin conditions just like it can help thrush, plaque, and tartar buildup. You know, it's one of those old-timer home remedies. I'm desperate, so I'm about ready to try anything."

"I know, girl, but let's maybe look at some other things." I said, trying to encourage her. "I'll start doing some Internet research, and we'll see what we can come up with in the next day or so. Until then just keep cold-hosing him as much as you can to keep him comfortable."

"I'll try, but if we haven't come up with anything by Wednesday, I'm starting the mouthwash treatment."

I laughed knowing good and well my dear friend was serious. Since moving to upstate South Carolina from south Mississippi, Erin's horse Pacer had been struggling with skin trouble every summer, and even though it was only the middle of spring, his skin was already irritated.

With the first signs of summer, the hair on Pacer's lower legs would stand on end, suggesting the beginning stages of rain rot. Gradually the inflammation and itch would increase as his upper legs and chest became affected.

He would start by nibbling at his ankles. He was soon scratching his knees and upper legs. By the time summer peaked, Pacer would spend his days ardently biting at his chest and looking for other ways to satisfy his itch. No fence post was safe. He'd center one on his chest, lean in, and rub. On hot days he'd take up residence in the door frame of the barn and violently scrape his neck against the boards while stripping every strand of hair from his mane.

I can't even list every treatment we tried.

Tea tree oil shampoos were time intensive, inconvenient, and helped very little. Bath day relieved a small amount of the itch, but by the time the next day's southern heat arrived, Pacer was back to his favorite place in the barn.

Baby oil soothed his skin and made one killer mess—especially on a horse who appreciates the value of a good roll. Ointments were the same and yielded results that were messy at best and a waste of money at worst.

After these and countless other failed attempts to treat Pacer's symptoms, Erin and I changed our thought process and began to research allergies. His issue was something that started only after the family's move to South Carolina. Ceratopogonidae (gnats, biting midges, sand flies, no-see-ums, punkies, and so forth) had a bad name in our area, so we looked into it.

Erin found an article that identified equine allergic reactions from saliva in the midge's bite and decided to go heavy on the fly spray for a while. Spending between fifteen and twenty dollars per bottle and averaging one bottle each week added up, but it definitely helped Pacer. Rubbing in the door of the barn eased up a bit, and the fence posts were tamped back straight. The problem wasn't completely solved, but we were headed in the right direction.

After a full season and a ten-year supply of empty bottles, we knew there had to be one last piece to the puzzle. If people can have allergies and horses can have allergies, isn't there a way to treat horses the same way you treat people? Internally. After a couple of phone calls to the vet and flipping through the pages of an equine supplement catalog, Erin hoped she had finally found her answer.

The new antihistamine investment paid off. After using it for just a couple of days, the hair on Pacer's legs began to lie flat, and for the first time, he spent a day milling around the pasture without visiting the barn once. For the whole summer, Pacer licked up his daily dose of meds and trotted off to do what horses do best—eat.

There's a story in the Bible about a man who, like Pacer, was being torn up by something on the inside that ended up destroying him on the outside. The man was Cain.

Cain was the first child born into the world and the oldest son of Adam and Eve. Like his father, Cain was a farmer and worked the land. His younger brother Abel was a shepherd. After the two brothers each made a sacrifice, God looked with favor on Abel but not Cain.

The Bible isn't clear why. Perhaps it was the spirit in which Cain made his sacrifice, or maybe he withheld the best portions for himself. Regardless of the circumstance, the older brother's jealousy grew into anger that eventually gave in to rage.

Overwhelmed by fury, Cain killed his brother.

The first murder in history resulted from Cain's refusal to admit he had done wrong in the eyes of the Lord, and jealous anger shaped his actions.

Holding on to painful emotions can do the same to us. Not just jealousy but also hurt, depression, guilt, grief, loneliness, regret, and sadness are just a few of the emotions we must learn to handle effectively. Trying to wash our feelings away with busyness won't work. Burying those emotions under layers of fake happiness won't solve the problem, and avoiding real relationships with those who want to share our lives is useless too.

Healing can only happen when we seek the Lord's comfort, love, and forgiveness and allow Him to restore us from the inside out.

> If you, LORD, kept a record of sins, Lord, who could stand? But with you there is forgiveness, so that we can, with reverence, serve you. I wait for the LORD, my whole being waits, and in his word I put my hope.
>
> Psalm 130:3-5

12

Splashin'

Marquise and I are quite unpopular at water crossings. What looks like a simple stream, creek, or for that matter, a water puddle is in fact huge entertainment for Marquise. He loves water, and I mean *loves* it. I honestly think he'd stand in the water for hours if we had a pond or a creek in the pasture.

When we're trail riding on hot summer days, he promptly assumes the responsibility of cooling himself anytime we cross water. Down goes the nose, up goes the foot, and we both get wet. He splashes the water on, and I scrape it off.

One day we were playing in the New River after the Virginia Highlands Endurance Challenge, and Marquise truly proved himself to be a water horse. He had such a tremendous time splashing around that by the time I was finally able to drag him back up the bank, we were both soaked from ear to tail and head to toe.

This problem is something we've worked on diligently in order to not disturb those around us, including my riding buddy Daphne, whose horse detests the water. Whenever I ride with her, we have a water-crossing system. She and Eclipse enter the water first—timidly I must add. Eclipse sniffs the water, sometimes tastes it, and only on the rarest of occasions will he be so brave as to take a sip.

After feigning an interest in the water long enough to satisfy Daphne, he's had enough and leaves the water as quickly as possible. During Eclipse's brief charade, Marquise stands, not so patiently, on the bank and waits his turn to play. Picture a young child just old enough to walk, yet a lover of water, clapping his hands, stamping his feet, and encouraging

Mommy to hurry up and put on his water wings. Now translate that excitement into horse terms.

At one time I attempted to correct Marquise's water-loving antics. I tried pulling his head up, smacking him on the shoulder, shifting my weight, and even not allowing him to enter the water at all. Then I realized this behavior is one of the quirks that makes Marquise special to me. If he wants to play, is there really any harm in it?

What makes you unique? All of us have distinctive characteristics. Some of us are like the spirited Arabian longing for adventure while others reflect the quiet dependability of a Quarter Horse. Perhaps your friends think fondly of you as the old mule whose steadiness has carried them over the rockiest parts of their lives. All of us are unique and have characteristics that make those around us either laugh or cringe.

What's most important is understanding and embracing the fact that you are uniquely you—created by God with the purpose of playing a specific role in His marvelous plan. Just as the veterinarian, farrier, and horse owner all work together for the health of the horse, so must we all work together as unique parts of the body of Christ.

Remember, love yourselves and each other. Our uniqueness is a gift from God, and we are all made perfect in His likeness. And by the way, if you come across a rider and a chestnut horse splashing away at a water crossing, it's just me and my water horse.

> I praise you because I am fearfully and wonderfully made; your works are wonderful, I know that full well. My frame was not hidden from you when I was made in the secret place, when I was woven together in the depths of the earth. Your eyes saw my unformed body; all the days ordained for me were written in your book before one of them came to be.
>
> Psalm 139:14-16

13

Compassion for the Lost

Alabama is home, yet I've become shamelessly enamored with the beauty and comfort of South Carolina. The Palmetto State is divided into three main regions: the low country, the midlands, and the upstate.

The low country was our home for a time, but Jeff and I chose to settle down in the upstate. Here I have the opportunity to frequent an extraordinary feature of South Carolina's topography, the mountains. From the front porch of my home, I can admire the renowned Blue Ridge Mountains. Their spine stretches through North Carolina, but a sufficient amount of the foothills reaches into the upstate, so I boldly claim their grandeur as my own. The trails that lead through their peaks and valleys remain undisclosed to most, but for me they are a neighboring treasure.

Competing against the notable reputations of the upstate and the low country, the often-forgotten midlands are unique in their own right. Whether on an endurance ride or a pleasurable trail outing, I've enjoyed the opportunity to ride there on occasion. Akin to thick golden snakes, the sandy trails in this area coil and twist around the thick pine trees. During the summer they act as solar panels and soak up the sun's heat with a hunger. Though not steep or technical, the trails there can trap even a seasoned rider who arrives unprepared.

Through dedication and tenacity, Theresa had her chance to compete in the midlands at the American Endurance Ride Conference National Championships. She qualified on her horse Jamag Tinian, "Jedi." I was going as her official crew.

Excitement in the endurance community and among our friends grew as the date drew near. This event promised to be well-organized and enjoyed by crew and riders alike. While I hurriedly prepared to leave, I was giddy about the vendors, the local band, and something I had never seen before—a big-screen TV posting real-time leaderboard statistics.

As usual when I have a fun horse-filled weekend planned, work got in the way, and my departure was delayed by several hours. I'd hoped to arrive early on Thursday to watch the hundred-mile top ten riders cross the finish line and sulked when I realized I would get there several hours after sunset. Top riders would already be off the trail.

Hours later and under cover of night, I turned my car toward the entrance of the H. Cooper Black Recreation Area. Glow sticks illuminated the trees ahead as a sign that horses and riders would soon be passing. All of my senses were on high alert. I rolled down my window, turned off the radio, and listened intently for the familiar sound of rhythmic hoofbeats.

Moments later the first pair came into view. Misty eyed with admiration, I watched the valiant team move out fearlessly on the shadowy trail. With a steady mount beneath her, the girl offered me a happy smile and spirited wave, and I cheered her bravery as she and her horse faded into the deep blackness beyond the beam of my headlights.

Nearing camp I scanned the trees for any directional markers but found none. Beginning to feel apprehensive, I called Theresa. She provided me with what *she* thought was an adequate description of the turn and abruptly hung up the phone. In an instant the comforting warmth of the glow sticks disappeared, and the dark ominous pines closed in. Their branches clawed the sides of my car and sent a bone-chilling fear down my spine as the cool night air whispered hauntingly in my ears.

I'd driven too far.

I made a quick three-point turn, prayed I wouldn't get stuck in the sand, and sped away from the eerie darkness.

Relief rushed through me when the campsite came into view. I parked next to Theresa's rig and hurried to find my friends at the vet area. The hustle and bustle was electric. Horses and riders anxiously waited for the out timer to allow them onto the trail, and crews worked feverishly to cool horses before presenting them to the vets. After an exchange of quick hellos and hugs, I made my way to the leaderboard to catch up on the race statistics. First through fifth places had been decided, and the remainder of the top ten were still out on the trail.

Then I heard the news. Someone was missing. The deep chill in my bones returned. I was just lost in those woods and was well aware of their threat. In search of answers, I questioned those around me.

Ride Management was well-prepared and knew the answers. Natalie, a rider from my area, had never passed a checkpoint seven miles out on the trail. She'd left well before dark, and now it was several hours into the night. Cell phone service was unreliable at best, and volunteers had gone to search on horseback and in utility vehicles. As a precaution the local sheriff had been alerted in case additional search-and-rescue help should be needed.

I'd only met Natalie a couple of times. We conditioned our horses on the same set of trails and often engaged in friendly conversation. A charming smile and welcoming laugh easily masked what a determined rider she was, but toughness aside she was in the dark, alone, and evidently lost. Concern for the missing horse and rider spread, and without a horse to join the search, I was useless. Stuck in camp I waited for news of her safe return.

Hours later the tension in my shoulders melted when I caught a glimpse of Natalie's uninjured horse being led back to its corral. The team had fought their battle against the darkness and won. However, after the excitement waned, my anxiety crept in—again.

How often are we concerned with the lost? I don't mean the physically lost, but the spiritually lost. When someone we know is spiritually lost, do we feel like it's a big deal—as in a matter of life or death? Or are we complacent and do nothing while their souls slip away without knowing the healing power of God's all-sufficient grace and forgiveness?

At this ride volunteers immediately came forward to look for the missing rider. They needed to know she was okay. Why then, with something as important as a person's soul, do we shy away from our responsibility to share God's love and the gospel?

> For I am not ashamed of the gospel, because it is the power of God that brings salvation to everyone who believes: first to the Jew, then to the Gentile.

> Romans 1:16

14

Content Where You Are

I listened courteously while Jen went on for what seemed like forever about her most recent perfect training ride. She and Jasper made a great team, had covered several miles that hot summer day, and were heading into the fall endurance season fit and ready to go. Finally she took a break. "Enough about me. How are you and Marquise?"

"I'm great," I answered. "Work is great. Jeff and I are really busy with work, so I just don't have time to ride. It's okay though. I really don't like riding when it's this hot anyway."

Lies, lies, lies.

What I really wanted to say was, *Actually, I'm not great. I work too much, and some days I'm just really happy Jeff and I haven't killed each other. I'd love to call you to go ride and would be happy to brave any kind of weather, but it's really a challenge to be able to fit a good ride into my schedule.*

I can't tell you *how* many times I've put on this pretty face just because it's what people expect.

Some days I'm so completely overwhelmed that I don't know what to do with myself, all the while my very expensive therapist sits in the pasture waiting for me to not cancel one of my mental therapy sessions. Most days I'm not lucky enough to ride, but simply stroking his bronze coat helps melt away my tension.

One day I was feeling more frazzled than usual from another crazy day and decided my nerves couldn't wait until I got home. I needed to vent right then, so I picked up the phone and called my friend Stephanie. She was all ears.

I wanted to scream into the phone, but I didn't have the energy, and so I whined, "All I want to do is go ride. I don't want to set any land-speed records. I don't even care about having a top-ten endurance horse. *All* I want to do is have Marquise fit enough to complete the distance healthy and happy so we can both have a fun weekend, *but* I can't even find time to condition for that. Something *always* pops up at work, and then I come home to a stack of bills and overflowing laundry. It's depressing to try to make time for myself because when I do, all of the grown-up stuff gets in the way."

Stephanie, my brutally honest and spiritually grounded friend, patiently listened to my moaning as I threw myself quite an elaborate, all-expense-paid pity party. Simmering down, I waited for her to validate my feelings with something that began with, "Poor Amber..." That's not what I got.

"Praise God." Her deliberate and quiet words shocked me back to reality.

"Huh?"

"Praise God. If you don't praise Him, the rocks will cry out instead. That's what it says in Scripture. He gives us boundless love, and in return all He asks for is our praise—no matter our situation in life. How can you expect to grow in your relationship with Christ if you never have a bad day?"

Okay, this isn't what I need right now, I thought. I was as confused as ever. Was she telling me that even though I was unhappy with my situation, I was supposed to praise God? Was praising God during hardship and difficulty when He gained the *most* glory? It would be so easy for me to praise God in a different situation. If I didn't have to work, I could praise God. If I had plenty of money, I could praise God. And, oh yeah, if I had a housekeeper so I could ride all day, I could be a walking worship wagon, but that's not my situation.

I'm supposed to praise God now, not once I get where I want to be.

Later that evening, I spent some quiet time on the porch reflecting on my conversation with Stephanie when God reminded me of a story. He knew it was the perfect one to lend some clarity to my situation. It was Jesus' parable of the loaned money.

In this story a man was going on a journey. Before he left he entrusted portions of money to three of his servants, each in accordance with his abilities. While the master was gone, two of them sought to please him, so they wisely invested the money. The third man didn't want to risk losing the money, so he buried it in a hole in the ground.

After the master returned home, the servants who had invested their portions proudly returned the money along with the interest they had earned. With this the master was overjoyed and rewarded them for their efforts by blessing them with much more. When the third presented only what was left with him, the master grew angry and judged him for being self-centered and unwilling to risk his reputation. That servant was stripped of what little he had and cast away.

When I applied this lesson to myself, I was shocked. I realized that I was the self-centered third servant. I was thinking of myself and what I wanted out of life rather than trying to make the most of the small things that God had already entrusted to me. Of course it's easy to praise God when things are going great—when the laundry is caught up, bills are paid, work is easy, and there's plenty of time to ride. Unfortunately that's not when all eyes are on me. It's when things aren't going great that people look at me and question how I'm going to respond.

More often than not, it's difficult for me to give God the kind of praise He deserves. I just hope to learn that if I invest the blessings He's given me, praise Him at all times, and anxiously await His return, I'll realize I've been blessed beyond measure.

> Though the fig tree does not bud and there are no grapes on the vines, though the olive crop fails and the fields produce no food, though there are no sheep in the pen and no cattle in the stalls, yet I will rejoice in the LORD, I will be joyful in God my Savior.
>
> Habakkuk 3:17-18

15

I Once Was Lost

"Ten o'clock? That works for me. See you then." A grin tugged at the corners of my mouth as I clicked off my phone and reached for my boots. Nothing could top a much-needed ride on this beautiful watercolor kind of day. With only a few weeks to go before our next endurance ride, Daphne and I knew this was one of our last opportunities to condition the horses.

The truck windows were down as I drove through the mountains and breathed deeply of the cool breeze swirling though the cab. The air was therapeutic and calming. Someone burned yard debris down in the valley, and the smoky smell of fall tickled my nose.

After I reached the parking area and unloaded, I brushed the dust from Marquise's coat while Daphne and I engaged in friendly chatter. We talked, but my mind wandered. *When should I ask?*

"The trails are going to be busy today," Daphne mentioned as she held Eclipse's hoof and wiggled his boot back and forth until it slipped over his heel. "Days like today bring the mountain bikers out like crazy. Do you think we should avoid Ridgeline Trail?"

This is my chance. "Actually I was wondering what you thought about maybe trying some new trails?" I ducked behind Marquise and pretended to pick out his hoof to avoid seeing her raise her eyebrows.

"Are you kidding?"

"No?" It came out as more of a question than the definitive answer I'd prepared. Truth be told, I'd stayed up late the night before going over my map in hopes of finding new trails to give us a good workout and the opportunity to explore.

"After what happened last time?"

"Okay, you're right. Last time didn't turn out so great." I thought back to our last trail ride when I was allowed to explore and reluctantly agreed with Daphne that maybe it was more important to exercise the horses than to seek out a new frontier. My spirits deflated slightly as I finished tacking up with a little less gusto and sadly tossed the map back into the trailer.

By the time I was double-checking my girth, Daphne had already tacked up, booted her horse, and was waiting patiently astride Eclipse. "Do you really want to explore?" Daphne asked when she noticed my pouty lip.

"Can we?"

"What if we ride our regular loop backwards?"

I don't know if it was her offer or the witty way she teased me in her English accent, but I perked up immediately. I would take adventure any way I could get it.

I threw a leg over the saddle, and we turned the horses toward the woods. Even though it was our usual loop, riding it in reverse brought me a fresh new excitement. Fighting to stay a nose ahead of his friend, Marquise made me laugh out loud as he lengthened his stride inch by inch and fought to pull the reins from my hands.

The trail descended to a creek bottom, and I welcomed the cool, damp air on the back of my neck. Dropping his head for a long drink, Marquise allowed me the reprieve I needed to roll the tension from my shoulders and rest my cramped hands. After the break both horses lunged up the bank and returned to a borderline uncontrollable gait.

Stride for stride the four of us moved and breathed as one. The mass of horse and human ate up the trail like a hungry beast—until we rounded a bend. Looming ahead of us stood one of the biggest and longest hill climbs of the day. I'd never seen it from this angle and hadn't considered the test it would be to go up instead of down.

"Let's see what they've got," I called to Daphne as Marquise pranced in place and stamped his feet.

"You're crazy but, sure, why not. Take off. I'll see you at the top!"

Marquise was elated and didn't stop to ask if I was sure about my quite out-of-character decision. In an instant he sprang forward. Once my stomach caught up with my body, I gathered my wits, dropped my heels, and focused on staying balanced long enough to make it to the top. We flew up the hill as my world blurred through my eyelashes.

Breathless and trembling, Marquise and I struggled to regain our composure while we waited for Daphne and Eclipse to join us. Almost a full minute later, Eclipse's white ears came into view as he and Daphne crested the hill. His gait was oddly irregular, and I quickly understood why we had won the race so easily.

In the excitement Eclipse had overreached and caught his front hoof boot. Now, held on by only a couple pieces of Velcro, it flopped hopelessly around his ankle. We had faced boot failure before and were no strangers to the situation. Daphne maintained her optimism and cheerfully hopped off to straighten the mess her mount had made.

She wiggled and tugged each part of the boot, turning it over in her hands. "We've got a problem."

"The screw?"

"Yep. That's not good, is it?"

We'd tried every boot on the market, and even though these were the best, they had one weakness. Stressed just right, a screw could pull right through the plastic and render the boot useless for the rest of the ride.

The boot was too far gone to be fixed on the trail, and the beginning of a great ride was now the end of a great ride. We were down but refused to be beaten. Daphne stowed the ineffective piece of gear in her saddlebag, and we set off again—slightly impaired by Eclipse and his bare hoof.

We managed just fine for several miles. Where the terrain allowed it, we moved out, and where it got rocky, we slowed the pace. Then it happened. I saw the handcrafted sign for Table Rock Trail. It beckoned to me like a bone to a hungry dog, and I couldn't resist shooting a pleading look Daphne's way.

"Go ahead," she offered with a laugh. "You and Mr. Big Shot, go check it out and then double back to catch up with us. You're going much faster, so I'll see you in a couple of minutes."

I turned Marquise's head in our new direction, released the reins, and without a second thought, he picked up a happy canter and carried me off into the unknown. But was I alone? Feeling like I was entering a ghost town, the lonely rustling leaves began to welcome me eerily, and uneasiness followed me from behind.

Marquise sensed my apprehension. Our relaxed canter through the woods turned into a series of seat checks as he spooked from one side of the trail to the other.

Enough of this.

A hard right rein turned us around, and a minute or so of galloping and lunging over rocks brought us back to the spot where I had left Daphne and Eclipse.

We both breathed a sigh of relief as his strong steady trot carried us to where I expected to find our friends. Instead we met a crossroad, and the truth of the situation became apparent. I realized not only was I usually the follower on these training rides, but we had also never done this loop backward.

Nothing looked familiar. I made a guess, and we went right. Surely I would catch up to Daphne any moment.

Darn! Another crossing.

I listened intently for any kind of sound breaking the stillness of the woods but heard nothing. Next I searched the ground for signs of a horse with only three boots and glumly realized the middle of a drought was not the best time to look for hoof prints on packed trails.

All right, I'm going have to guess—again.

I was hopelessly lost. The one thing I could have depended on was the map—and it was back at the trailer. Marquise and I wandered for another mile or two before the trail finally opened up to reveal the trailers. It was good to be back.

How many times have we set out with our own plan and agenda and failed to realize that we weren't equipped well enough to make the best decisions?

Life is like that. It's full of choices—fast or slow, right or left, good or bad. Although our choices can vary, they all have one thing in common. Every decision we make has consequences. Sometimes the effects of our decisions are good, like when we give a hug or spend time listening to someone who needs us. Other times our decisions cause pain to someone we care about or cause ourselves to suffer physically or emotionally.

God doesn't want us to be scared or question which way to go as we travel through this wonderful journey called life. That's why He speaks to us through His Word—the Bible. It never leads us astray and is always good. The only way to make the best decisions for our lives is to follow the map God provides and remember when we head out on the trail of life, don't leave it behind.

> All Scripture is God-breathed and is useful for teaching, rebuking, correcting and training in righteousness.
>
> **2 Timothy 3:16**

16

Dirty All Over Again

Marquise and the goats' feed buckets swung from my hands as I neared the gate for the evening feeding and took inventory of the beautification work that awaited me. Seven flies hovered near the corners of Marquise's eyes, four on one and three on the other. Tiny streams of equine tears slid down the dish on his face before drying into a crust near his nostrils, and three large wind knots claimed territory in his mane. Splotches of sweat dotted his shoulders, and flecks of dried salt draped his rump in an Appaloosa-style blanket.

Marquise was a mess, but every night during feeding time was the perfect opportunity to attempt a reversal of everything the summer humidity and bugs had done to him. With his nose buried deep in a bucket of soaked alfalfa pellets, he was much less likely to express a contrary opinion. As long as the single cup of food swimming around in an excessive amount of water held out, his highness let me pick his feet, dig the curry into the crunchy salt, and carefully untangle each strand of golden mane. The gooey stuff in the corner of his eyes demanded a quick yet strategic swipe of the towel before he licked the last fleck of dinner from the side of the bucket.

The moment the final bit of reconstituted legume disappeared, he headed for the goats' buckets to give them the official Marquise "tongue scrub." After just one step, he paused at the salt lick to work its corners and then rested his lips lightly on the surface of the water in the trough to take several long sips. Through all of this, he stayed clean and—as always—stunning.

Then the countdown to the "de-grooming" process began.

Marquise stepped back out into the pasture to signify the return to his domain. Here dirt and caked mud outdid fly spray in treating itchy spots, and a tangled mane was a prestigious sign that pixies had chosen him to ride about in the evenings. (My mom told me that's how wind-knots came to be.) Clean time officially ended. The results of my preening and cleaning lasted mere moments before it gave way to the horse's rolls and grunts. Marquise's routine was intentional, precise, and painful to watch.

His lounging spot was the same every night. Made up of the perfect mix of sand and dirt, it ground deeply into his coat. After two circles and a couple of paws with a front hoof, down he went. He didn't just cordially roll to treat his itches. No! It was an in-your-face, disrespectful, roll-on-both-sides, and then scrub-the-face-in-the-dirt kind of roll. Within minutes my nightly grooming unraveled. After addressing his left side, he sat up, blinked hard to get the dust out of his eyes, wrestled himself to his feet, shook, and repeated the whole process on the right.

He enjoyed it immensely. I could tell by his guttural groans during the process and by the way he hopped up and ran across the pasture enjoying a good bucking session. Once he was far enough away from the brushes, curries, and hoof pick, he relaxed and dropped his head into a lush patch of grass. Dirt clung to the places where fly spray hadn't dried, and the tips of his mane showed the beginning of tangles, but I still smiled as my happy red horse enjoyed his freedom.

As Christians we're free—free to live, free to make our own decisions, and free to return to sin after we get cleaned up. But is it right to abuse our freedom and God's grace?

Once we accept Christ as our Savior, our sins are cast away into a sea of forgetfulness, but why do we continue sinning? Is it because sin is easy or feels good, or is it because it helps us get something we want? I worked to clean Marquise up, because I knew he needed the fly spray, and I knew leaving his hair knotted would make it break, but what he wanted was the scratch of the dirty sand against his skin and the little mud patches above his eyes. For him it wasn't about what was good for him but about what *felt* right. To him acting like a horse felt right.

Acting like a sinner feels right for us, because sin is a part of our human nature. We are compelled to sin and do what feels good. Staying clean is actually contrary to what feels natural and easy. Amazingly enough Christ has cleansed us not just for today's sins but for all of our sins in the future.

I once heard that the definition of insanity is repeating the same action and expecting a different result. By that definition my routine of cleaning Marquise up every day is insanity, but when Christ rains down His love over our same old sins, it's the true definition of grace.

> What shall we say, then? Shall we go on sinning so that grace may increase? By no means! We are those who have died to sin; how can we live in it any longer? Or don't you know that all of us who were baptized into Christ Jesus were baptized into his death? We were therefore buried with him through baptism into death in order that, just as Christ was raised from the dead through the glory of the Father, we too may live a new life.

Romans 6:1-4

17

Common Thread

Though each equestrian discipline is unique in its own way, a common thread runs deeply through each one.

❧

The endurance crew works for very little pay—actually no pay. They wake up hours before dawn to double check girths and dose electrolytes. Probably at least once, they've rescued a rider from an exhaustion-induced disaster. The most dedicated crew will wipe a rider's dirt-streaked face with the hem of a white shirt, hand-feed a picky eater, and happily trot out a very sound horse for a very lame rider. When the ride is finally over, a good crew will massage sore muscles (equine and human alike), help break down camp, and on the way home, cheerfully hop out of the truck to change a tire on the side of the interstate.

❧

Before the first show of the season, the "horse-show mom" will take the truck and trailer in for maintenance. As soon as she gets them back home, she'll slip on her shorts, tie up her vintage eighties T-shirt, and proceed with waxing the trailer roof while listening to Katrina and the Waves belt out "Walking on Sunshine." Show weekend is packed full of grooming, braiding, walking, mucking, and feeding followed the next day by grooming, braiding, walking, mucking, and feeding. A horse-show mom will wear out a set of tires on a Sundowner in a summer by driving from one event to another to chase the dream of equine stardom.

❧

Her daddy searched high and low before he found that sweet palomino to carry his baby girl. When the pony's dewy brown eyes met his, he saw honesty and heard the promise the horse made with her heart. He took the palomino home and trusted her with his most precious possession.

That fall at the county fair, his baby girl's pigtails bounced in their pink ribbons, and her daddy beamed in a matching pink, starched button-up. He wore the color proudly even though his weathered hands holding the lead line had far more often folded down a blue collar. He didn't make a dime to invest that day, but he went home feeling like the richest man in the world.

Our day had started at four in the morning, and now it was again four a.m.—twenty-four hours later. My eyelids sagged and begged to close after dropping Marquise off at the emergency veterinary hospital. Theresa and I had a two-and-a-half-hour drive ahead of us to get back to camp, and the second time I crossed the double yellow line, I looked at her helplessly. "I need you to drive," I said. The night had been too much for me, and she was there to help me when I couldn't help myself.

On a windy, cold Friday night before Christmas, I heard those same words.

"I need you to drive." Erin's horse, Pacer, had gashed his hoof severely and required immediate veterinary attention. Erin didn't have a trailer, and like I'd always promised, I hooked up, drove to her house, loaded the injured horse, and off we drove.

What do these four stories have in common? They don't involve the same discipline, the same horse, or even the same people.

The commonality is that in all of the examples, someone is being a servant, not because there's something to gain and not because there is praise in the end, but because each one of these people truly put another's needs before their own.

The greatest example of a servant this world has ever seen is Jesus Christ. In His ministry He healed people, held children, and brought hope to mankind. When He was tired, He pressed on, never seeking glory for Himself.

All of this was for what? In the best case scenario, He was unappreciated, but in reality He faced death and was crucified. He didn't have to do this, but He considered our need for salvation greater than His life and willingly offered it up in exchange for our souls.

Being a humble servant, though lowly, is a tremendous calling and one that was worthy of our Lord Himself.

> Do nothing out of selfish ambition or vain conceit. Rather, in humility value others above yourselves.
>
> **Philippians 2:3**

18

The Armor of God

"No foot, no horse." Jeremiah Bridges of Great Britain coined this phrase in the mid-eighteenth century, and since then it has become one of the truest statements ever made regarding horses. Since the horse's domestication thousands of years ago, hoof protection has traveled full circle, and the horse has done the same.

Horses once roamed freely. Their hard hooves protected the delicate internal structures of the foot and carried them many miles daily in search of food and water. As horses became a part of civilization, their roles changed significantly. They no longer spent their days traveling in search of food and water but were asked to bear the weight of packs, carts, and war-hungry riders. Horses' hooves began to suffer when the horses were relocated to colder, wetter climates and were kept in more confined areas.

These changes heralded the era of hoof protection. The first hoof boot was fashioned from leather or rawhide, and the horseshoe was forged from iron or bronze. They both offered protection from weaknesses caused by domesticated living, stalling, and the lack of a natural self-trimming environment.

No longer a necessity for day-to-day living, the common horse now fills the role of partner and loyal friend. Whether in the show ring or on the trail, "no foot, no horse" resonates through every rider's thoughts after just one lame step. It's for this reason that many riders and owners would rather spend money on hoof protection to prevent lameness rather than try to fix it after the fact.

I know this better than most and as well as many. Marquise was show bred and stall kept during many of the years he would have developed the kind of hoof necessary for endurance riding, so I do what I can to protect him. My pre-ride hoof regimen took quite a bit of extra time, and that was why I always tried to beat Daphne to the trailhead.

⚬⚬⚬⚬⚬⚬

The morning sun warmed the seat of my favorite riding tights and reflected off the gravel parking lot as I cradled Marquise's front hoof between my knees. Using an old hand-me-down rasp, I trimmed the slightest bit of length off with just a few licks to the toe. After cleaning his hoof with a hoof pick, I reached behind me for the black, plastic hoof boot.

Noticing the worn tread, I made a mental note to order another pair. With a push, a tug, and a toe tap on the ground, Marquise's hoof slipped into the boot's protective shell. He immediately weighted it and happily lifted his opposite bare foot from the parking lot's jagged gravel.

My mind wandered to the boots horses wore centuries ago to protect their war-weary feet. Then I thought about the armor the brave warhorses wore into battle—the heavy metal plates that covered the neck and chest, the padded cloth for the hindquarters, and the head armor, which was often decorated with horns or spikes to create a likeness to the fabled unicorn.

Each piece, specifically fashioned by a metalsmith, protected the mounts as they fearlessly carried their riders deep into the heart of battle. An unarmored horse would have faced a quick demise.

So why then are we so quick to face the wars of our life without the protection we need and are supplied with freely?

Each one of us faces personal battles every day. Maybe it's a battle against jealousy or the inability to tame a lashing tongue. Negativity, depression, and anger can burn inside us as a battle that can't be seen and is often overlooked. The unseen forces of evil lurk and desire to see us fall.

Therefore, we must arm ourselves daily for a battle not of this world, and thank the Lord who has provided us with everything we need. The belt of truth and the breastplate of righteousness must be in place, and our feet should be fitted with the readiness of the gospel of peace. The shield of faith, the helmet of salvation, and, most importantly, the sword of the

Spirit are not only protection but are critical when we're on the offense and battling the evil one.

Our horses need protection when they're trotting down the trail, jumping a cross-country course, or packing us through the wilderness, and though we all have a different way of taking care of their feet, we all know "no foot, no horse."

We should take this thought to heart. The foundation for our lives should be a right relationship with Jesus Christ. Without protecting it against Satan's evil schemes by wearing our spiritual armor, our foundation can be shaken. Just as a horse without a foot isn't much good, an unprotected heart for Christ is just as useless.

> Finally, be strong in the Lord and in his mighty power. Put on the full armor of God, so that you can take your stand against the devil's schemes. For our struggle is not against flesh and blood, but against the rulers, against the authorities, against the powers of this dark world and against the spiritual forces of evil in the heavenly realms. Therefore put on the full armor of God, so that when the day of evil comes, you may be able to stand your ground, and after you have done everything, to stand. Stand firm then, with the belt of truth buckled around your waist, with the breastplate of righteousness in place, and with your feet fitted with the readiness that comes from the gospel of peace. In addition to all this, take up the shield of faith, with which you can extinguish all the flaming arrows of the evil one. Take the helmet of salvation and the sword of the Spirit, which is the word of God.
>
> Ephesians 6:10-17

19

Little Tree

Theresa and I have a thing about horse names and what they can mean for a rider. Dash might spin and leave you in the dirt. Jet Fuel is probably going to be a little hard to control—but only for the first fifty miles or so. Killer, well that name speaks for itself. Horses named after natural disasters such as cyclones, hurricanes, and volcanoes also tend to make me hesitate to hop on.

If I'd been applying that theory to choosing a trail, Marquise and I probably would've passed the turn onto Thomas Cemetery Road. Its name lacked the appeal of Fawn Lake Loop or Vista Trail, both of which sounded so friendly and appealing, but for some reason I made the turn anyway. The packed gravel path didn't disappoint either of us. It was wide and had an alluring curve that led us down to a creek bottom—perfect for a relaxed easy canter.

The trees and scrub brush dotted the periphery as my trusty steed and I wound through the woods. As we approached the trail's namesake, the Thomas Family Cemetery, I chose to gather in the reins. The few gravestones were surrounded by a log fence and above them was a sign that read:

> No Pain No Grief
> No Anxious Fear
> Can Reach Our Loved Ones
> Sleeping Here

A sweet peacefulness rested in the treetops as we enjoyed our stop. After pausing a few moments to pay our respects, I nudged Marquise forward and asked for our previous canter. He politely refused, and for whatever reason, I conceded. It took only a few steps before I completely relaxed in the saddle and swayed comfortably in rhythm with his hooves.

If I'd been insistent in my canter request, I would have missed what I now refer to as my favorite tree. About five feet off the trail, stood the most unique pine tree I've ever seen. The trunk grew up from the ground for about three feet and then made a sharp turn down toward the ground. Once it touched the ground, it curved back up and grew as straight as an arrow toward the sun just as one would expect. This wasn't a small tree either. At about forty inches in diameter, it had been living with this unique shape for quite some time. Surely it had given more than one passerby reason for pause.

As a child would name shapes in the clouds, I began thinking of how I could best explain this to Jeff when I got home. I finally came up with the perfect illustration—a golf club. He would be able to picture that for sure. The looping of the trunk created the club's face, and the part that returned to normal made the shaft. Well, it was either a golf club or a snail with a really, really long neck.

Why did it do that? Why did it curl in such a crazy way while none of the surrounding vegetation looked out of the ordinary and nothing else touched it?

I can only assume something happened years before that either damaged it or acted on it in a way that altered its growth. No matter what caused its strange shape, the little tree continued to grow. It still bears the scars of the trauma, but today it's strong and thriving.

At some point in our lives, each of us will have things happen that will scar us and change us, and we'll have to decide if those things are going to kill us or just change how we grow. Losing a job, a friendship, or even a special horse are all traumatic events. It can be easy to let those things steal our joy and zest for life or cause us to put up walls against being hurt in the future. Instead of retreating into our own protection or just dying inside, we have to rely on the Lord's strength to help us keep growing.

Like the tree in the woods, our experiences change us and make us different. This is okay. The life events we endure make us unique. They are the same events that make others stop and question how we had the strength to keep pressing on.

Every time I pass that tree in the woods and ponder its growth, I'm reminded of God's promise. He will supply me with the strength I need to get through each day no matter what adversity it brings.

> So do not fear, for I am with you; do not be dismayed, for I am your God. I will strengthen you and help you; I will uphold you with my righteous right hand.
>
> **Isaiah 41:10**

20

The Least of These

Erin and I sat in my truck, blocked by the three-strand, electric-tape gate. We'd turned into the drive and now sat staring at a big palomino and white mini that seemed to be eating off the same blade of grass. It was cold, but they were blanketed and obviously well fed. As my diesel idled in the driveway, their heads lifted. They were more interested in the fresh hay packed in the bed of my truck than the bare ground.

"Can you get the gate?" Poised with the door open and ready to hop out, Erin had read my mind before the words left my mouth.

"Ha! Easier said than done. Take it slow 'cause you're going to be slinging mud getting out of here." She laughed and stepped wide around the deep mud after deciding against the jump she'd planned.

She walked in front of the bumper and gathered each of the three electric handles to open the gate. I eased through with my heavy load while the two horses planned their attack on the feed truck that bravely entered their territory.

An abandoned house in front of us occupied the center of the horses' scant pasture. White paint peeled from the sashing around lifeless windows, and rich green ivy crept up the sides of the crumbling brick walls. Growing wild without fear of an annual trim, arrogant branches on the shrubbery stretched the length of the porch in defiance of their once-manicured lives.

For a moment we wondered which way to go, but once we looked to the right, it was apparent. Through another gate I saw an old barn with a blue tarp tacked over the door as a makeshift awning. Outside what was once a hitching post was now an organizing station for a compilation of shovels, rakes, wheelbarrows, and buckets. Nearby a pile of sawdust lay protected under plastic from the winter chill. As we rolled closer, beautiful hounds from behind chain-link fences welcomed us with a melodious baying opus.

I'd never heard such a sound and found it soothing as the deep-chested timbre of bloodhounds mingled with the lighter tones of beagles. We'd just driven onto the property of a local hound rescue. As they ran to follow the truck, their red and brown coats shimmered in stark contrast to the bland dirt behind the fence. They were all healthy and strong. Although their physical needs were taken care of, it saddened me that they wouldn't spend the night sleeping at the foot of someone's bed.

Diane, the rescue manager, met us at the barn with a glowing smile and bubbling chatter. The lilt in her voice intrigued me. As she showed us to the barn, I saw that behind one of the dog runs was a tiny travel trailer that she clearly called home. While moving a few bales of old hay from one stack to another, I stole a look behind some tattered blankets, which were nailed up to block the cold night air from Diane's furry tenants. Each sneak peek rewarded me with bright eyes and happy tails.

I'd learned about Diane's need for hay from Daphne who volunteered at a local food crisis ministry. As a victim of the failing economy, Diane had come in to ask for help. She'd lost her job, and now the meager social security check she drew monthly supported her four-legged family almost one hundred percent. Her tiny stature as compared to the animals' hale and hearty frames told me they were eating far better.

Rain had been plentiful during the winter, but the ground still wasn't warm enough to produce grass for Diane's horses, and she was a few weeks short on hay. Thankful that Daphne had thought of me as someone who might be able to help, I immediately went to Erin who had been blessed with an excess. That's why we were unloading hay into a dilapidated barn turned hound home and pondering the happiness of the tiny woman who stacked it.

After emptying the truck bed and brushing out the loose stems, Diane stood by the tailgate with her hands stuffed deep in the pockets of her fleece pullover. With her brow wrinkled and an emotional veil shrouding her thoughts, she turned her gaze to the ground and searched for the appropriate words to thank us. In the seconds that ticked by, we stood speechless, not sure how to bring closure to our time together. Finally Diane looked up and said, "Do you want to see a picture of my horse?"

In no rush to leave, we climbed the three stairs that led into her humble home. On the wall hung a worn, framed picture of a polished rider turned out in impeccable white breeches and a black hunt jacket. The blonde's smile lured me to the green hill where she sat proudly astride an inky black bay.

"He was my field hunter, and he never dropped me once. We could be in the middle of taking a coop or a fence, and if I was even a touch off center, he'd move himself under me. He's buried right over there." Her aged delicate finger pointed to a pile of fresh dirt by the fence. "I lost him at thirty, and he'd been mine for twenty-six years."

Diane was a kindred spirit—in love with life and her animals. After years of caring for horses at several barns along the East Coast, her home was now a hound rescue in the foothills of the Blue Ridge Mountains. The luxury and prestige of the equine world and the money that flowed through it had been traded for the hearts of the least of these—an odd assortment of bloodhounds, bassets, and beagles. In something as simple as showing up with a load of fresh hay, I received a share of her blessing.

Although our Sunday afternoon had been interrupted by loading hay, driving to a stranger's home, and sharing what we had, Erin and I received the gift of knowing we'd not only cared for a needy palomino and a companion mini but also another soul.

How we treat the people around us—the sick, the broken, the hurting—is how we treat Jesus. When we love them, we love Him, and when we provide for their needs, we show thankfulness for our blessings. Love has a ripple effect, and what we do today will inevitably touch lives in ways we will never know.

> "For I was hungry and you gave me something to eat, I was thirsty and you gave me something to drink, I was a stranger and you invited me in, I needed clothes and you clothed me, I was sick and you looked after me, I was in prison and you came to visit me."
>
> Then the righteous will answer him, "Lord, when did we see you hungry and feed you, or thirsty and give you something to drink?

When did we see you a stranger and invite you in, or needing clothes and clothe you? When did we see you sick or in prison and go to visit you?"

The King will reply, "Truly I tell you, whatever you did for one of the least of these brothers and sisters of mine, you did for me."

Matthew 25:35-40

21

Who Are You?

There was no point in setting the alarm. My eyes were open long before the early morning sun first beckoned through the window. Quietly slithering from the bed, trying not to wake my husband or the dogs, I padded toward the kitchen for my morning coffee. I happily bypassed the laundry room and the chore of choosing clothes for the day. Three days ago I'd laid out the perfect outfit along with my special jewelry and boots.

After a cold splash of water on my face, I took a long drink of hot coffee, leaned closer to the mirror, and snagged the lone eyebrow hair that stood out wildly. *Gotcha!* I rubbed the sharp sting and blinked to clear my watering eyes. Hootie and Tully had crawled out of bed and curled up by my feet to sleepily watch my morning. "It's a big day, kids. I've got to look extra special."

My hair willingly conformed to the shape of a low, sleek ponytail, and the backs of my grandmother's pearl earrings settled into place. A quick blast of hairspray and coat of red lipstick finished off the look, and I headed toward the guest bedroom to gather my clothes. I first placed the boots into my black duffel. Next I packed my knee-high silk socks and a small assortment of toiletries. I grabbed the garment bag that had been packed days before, unzipped it to make sure nothing had spontaneously disappeared, counted the hangers, and closed it up.

I was ready.

"I'll be back soon," I said as I knelt down by the front door to scratch the dogs on the head. "We'll do dinner tonight. I hear your papa is going to grill us some steaks." They each offered an appreciative kiss on the cheek, and I stood and walked confidently out the door.

The show grounds had a voice all their own—at least it felt that way. There were so many horses milling around and warming up that the anxious calls couldn't be pinned on one single horse. The snorts, hoofbeats, and nickers seemed to bubble up from the ground that surrounded Maria and me at the trailer.

"Are you nervous?" Maria asked while I fumbled with another band for Marquise's mane.

"No. I just can't get these tiny braids right." Marquise's mane was down to his shoulders and was the trademark that earned him the barn name "Hollywood." "I don't think I'm going to be able to get these braids done without it looking like he has a hundred red cucumbers tied to his neck."

"You're absolutely right." Maria laughed at my struggle and stepped in to offer a solution. "Let me help."

"You've done these tiny braids before?"

"No, but I have another idea." With Maria's hand on the brush, the bristles sped through Marquise's mane with ease. "Did you put detangler on this?" Maria asked while trying to get a grip on the red, white, and gold strands.

"No. Can you not get a hold of it?"

"Not even a little bit. No wonder you were having such a hard time. Do you have any hair products in your bag? Gel? Mousse? Hairspray? Mud? Anything?"

I knew I'd packed that duffel with extra toiletries for a reason. "I sure do. Got it all right here. Pick your poison."

Maria dug through the bag of human hair products and settled on a can of Aqua Net, my go-to hairspray for the low sleek ponytail. She sprayed until the circling summer flies fell from the thick air—their wings cemented tightly by hair-product paralysis. Marquise looked like a reject from a low-budget, eighties music video, but it was just what Maria needed for her flying fingers to grab and go to work.

Two minutes later a beautiful running braid ran securely down Marquise's arching neck, and a tight knot sat neatly between his ears. All of a sudden, he flashed back to his show-ring days, puffed his chest, flared his nostrils, and pricked his ears.

Maria gave me a leg up and used a clean towel to shine the tips of my boots and wipe arena dust from Marquise's handsome face. We were ready.

There was almost no reason to make a stop at the warm-up arena. By the time we got there, Marquise was already damp from showing off an animated Arabian-style *passage*, and I was looking like I had chosen a mount way beyond my ability for a first dressage test. Still I decided to go ahead with the official warm-up and practiced my transitions for several minutes before Maria stopped me.

"You go at nine-ten. It's nine-oh-five. We'd better head to the arena." Maria's voice was calm and sure—the polar opposite of how I felt. We neared the arena, and I couldn't decide if I really belonged.

My polished dress boots showed no sign of wear, and my new, white, full-seat breeches fit like tailored gloves. The stock pin I wore indicated I was a dressage arena veteran, and my dog-hair-free dress coat fell comfortably across my shoulders. I *looked* like a dressage rider.

However, my synthetic English trail saddle showed a little salty sweat residue that I hadn't been able to scrub off. My stirrup irons had a few spots of rust (they were borrowed—I certainly didn't have English irons), and my fifteen-dollar, consignment-store bridle didn't look like the Havana-brown soft leather ones that my competitors sported.

In no time the bell rang, and I began my circle around the arena before entering. During these strides I firmly dropped my heels and planted the balls of my feet in the borrowed irons. A steel rod of confidence drove down my spine and through my hips, lifting my chin and squaring my shoulders. I bravely entered the arena at A, offered the judge a poised salute at X, and began my test.

I remembered everything—the transitions, how to ask for willing collection, and the quiet bump from the inside rein that dropped Marquise's head. We glided across the sand and executed a near-perfect final halt at our return to X. We'd absolutely rocked the United States Dressage Federation Introductory Level Test A, the simplest dressage test written. I gave Marquise a firm pat on the neck and Maria a thumbs-up. I began walking toward the stand where the judge had risen to her feet.

She spoke as I neared. "What a nice test and a lovely horse. What's his breeding?"

Oh, of course she doesn't know. She probably never sees Arabians since dressage is a world for warmbloods and Thoroughbreds. She's probably shocked he's so small. "He's an Arab." I said it with sincerity, conviction, and pride. My little red horse had held his ground against other horses whose long legs were made for the discipline.

"I know that. What's his breeding?"

I sensed annoyance. *His breeding? I'm lost.*

"Is he Polish, Egyptian, Russian…?"

I stared blankly and got the feeling this should've been an easy question. "Um…He's out of Huckleberry Bey." It really was the best and only answer I could come up with.

"Okay, thank you. That will be all." The judge dismissed me and sat down.

Marquise's breeding didn't matter that day, and it still doesn't, but it bothered me that I didn't have an answer. Though my face-to-face meeting with ignorance was brief, it made me curious enough to look it up.

Who are you? Good looks and performance aside, who are you really? Are you a rider? A teacher? A friend? A wife? A father? When it all boils down to what matters, it's not whether you have the most toys at the end of the game, the most ribbons at the end of the show, or the most cash at the end of your life. It matters where you found your identity through it all.

Sometimes it's easy to say, "I'm a Christian," but do you know what those words really mean and why that simple statement should have an impact on every fiber of your being? It means you were bought with a price and believe that price was the perfect innocent blood of Jesus Christ. You believe that Christ is all-forgiving and all-forgetting. You believe that your imperfections are made perfect through the grace of Christ, and it's by this grace that you've been given an eternal place in paradise.

So the next time someone asks who you are, make sure you know the answer.

> You are all children of God through faith, for all of you who were
> baptized into Christ have clothed yourselves with Christ.
>
> **Galatians 3:26-27**

22

Pride

I loved Sheree for her great idea—or at least I used to. She'd arranged for our riding group to spend the night in Big Barn in a state park where overnight camping wasn't allowed in exchange for a mere three hours of volunteered physical labor. With appreciation for the opportunity to do something few other people had the chance to do, the girls and I ecstatically packed our trailers. When morning arrived, forest rangers would split us into two groups and direct us to opposite sides of the park. Each group would work from nine to noon. This would be a breeze, and the rest of the afternoon would be free for riding.

The August morning heat thickened the air, but there was still plenty of excitement about the fun ride that would happen after our debt to the forest service was paid. Taylor and I had used weed eaters before, so we hopped in the truck that was headed south to clean up the entrance at the back of the park. The other group was taken to the front entrance. For three miserable hours, Taylor and I pushed lawnmowers through grass up to our knees, trimmed weeds around rocks only fit for rattlesnakes, and sweat buckets as we hauled limbs up a hill. When my weed eater sputtered and coughed, I wilted to the ground, thankful the ranger had driven off with the spare gas can. No matter what the other group was doing, I knew we were outworking them by far.

As the ranger drove us back to camp, I rubbed the volcanic blisters that had erupted from the palms of my hands. I used my dirty shirt to wipe my dirty face that was streaked with dirty sweat. Laughter rang through camp as we stepped out of the truck and took in the ocean of happy faces smiling our way.

"I told 'em!" Theresa laughed as she pointed to the grunge on my shirt

and the briars on my jeans. "We planted some shrubs, spread pine needles, and picked up trash, but I told 'em you'd somehow be out there trying to show us up. Looks like you did. How does it feel?"

"It feels great." I sunk to my knees and flopped face-first in the grass. It
was the happiest I'd been all day. "What's for lunch?"

"Oh, we already ate. We've been back for an hour and helped ourselves
to the sandwich fixings you brought to share. We were just talking about
saddling up for an afternoon ride. You in?"

"Ugh." The groan escaped more from my gut than my mouth. Could
I really find the energy to ride after this kind of morning?

"Get up, sissy." Theresa nudged my limp body with the toe of her boot
and offered me a cold Gatorade. "Chances like this don't come often, and
you'll never forgive yourself if you miss it."

I nodded my head even though the grass I lay on scrubbed the side
of my face. We were camped in one of the most beautiful state parks
around—where *The Last of the Mohicans* and *The Hunger Games* were
filmed. If I missed riding because I was too tired, I wouldn't be allowed
to call myself an endurance rider anymore, so I pushed myself up and sat
back on my heels. Could I or couldn't I?

"Pass me a sandwich. I'll eat it from right here on the ground, and then
we'll tack up." The group cheered my determination to enjoy a long ride,
and in truth I knew it had to be better than a nap in the back of a hot
horse trailer.

⟡

The late-summer air looked alive. The leaves crunched underfoot
and cushioned our horses' hooves as they swept over the trails. Marquise
strained against the bit, and I prided myself in simply being able to hold
on for the entire twelve-mile round trip.

Back in camp we groomed and fed the horses and made our way
over to the fire where Sheree's husband was grilling up some mighty fine
chicken. I stayed awake through dinner, but what I really wanted was a
shower and bed.

Walking through the sawdust in the aisle of Big Barn felt more like
trudging through a swamp bog as I made my way to the old stall that had
been converted to the bathhouse. I was tempted to drag the metal chair

from the corner over to the shower to let the hot water work on my worn-out bones and sore muscles.

My eyelashes fluttered with the weight of the day's labor and the awe-some trail ride, and I anxiously anticipated the steam that would soon be rolling off my shoulders. As the water sprayed from the showerhead, I waited behind the green tarp turned shower curtain. Soon the welcome warmth would fend off the cool draft that crept down from the rafters.

After several minutes I gave up. The hot water never made an appear-ance, so I suffered through an agonizing ice-cold splash shower. The soft-ness of the terry-cloth towel did what the shower couldn't and lulled me toward rest. My flip-flops flipped and flopped as I walked down the sawdust-lined aisle.

"Where are you going?" Theresa asked as I passed her with my towel-turbaned head bobbing in exhaustion.

"Bed."

"Um, are you going to hay your horse?"

"Ugh." For the second time that day, I felt like I'd been punched in the gut.

"Geez, I'll get him. You look pitiful." With that she turned down the aisle and disappeared into the darkness. I'd had enough of my pride for the day and was too tired to be guilt-tripped into running out behind her. I headed in the opposite direction and toward my trailer, curled up, and fell fast asleep before she made it to the corrals.

I wanted to be *that* person the rangers talked about for weeks—the one that gave a hundred and ten percent without complaining. If I worked hard enough, maybe next time our group wouldn't have to ask permission to come back. Instead maybe the rangers would invite us.

The plan didn't work out quite like that. After my shining three hours of glory, I almost missed the point of the whole weekend because I was so exhausted. For those few hours, I was focused on seeing who could work the hardest, pull the most weeds, or get the dirtiest, but that wasn't what it was about.

Our group wasn't allowed the privilege of camping in the forest so we could work ourselves to death and have a great trail ride. Instead it was so we could partner with the men and women of the forest service and show our appreciation for the safe trails they provide.

Work is hard, but it's rewarding. Regardless of whether it's our career, raising a family, or building a relationship, the Bible says we should work for the Lord and we should work together. Any aspect of our lives can benefit from the application of these principles. By asking these questions, it's easy to get started.

First, does the work I've chosen glorify God or me? If it's the latter, maybe I should choose something else or at least change my attitude.

Second, am I working to the best of my ability or am I being lazy because no one is watching?

Third, am I working with someone to help lighten their load or am I only interested in making myself look better?

If I had applied these principles sooner, my day spent in the forest may have been a little more enjoyable.

> He makes the whole body fit together perfectly. As each part does its own special work, it helps other parts grow, so that the whole body is healthy and growing and full of love.
>
> **Ephesians 4:16** NLT

23

Are You Prepared?

The sound of giggling woke me up, but I might have stayed in bed if I'd known the joke was on me.

"What's with the laughing, and where's the coffee?" Groaning from the previous morning's work in the forest, I stepped out of my trailer and settled my very sore moving parts onto a cooler.

"It's Marquise," Theresa said. "That horse has never missed a meal, and I know how he's making sure of it." She tried to stifle her giggles with gulps of too-hot coffee.

"Okay, what gives?" I asked. I was certain that it wasn't nearly as funny as everyone thought.

"Well, last night after I passed you in the hall, I threw out hay. Marquise and Sheik were the closest so I got to them first. Then I walked down to give some to Jedi, Eclipse, and Phoenix."

"And?"

"Well, I spent a few minutes down in the bottom corral just to double-check gates and water. By the time I made it back up to the barn, Marquise was fast asleep—with a mouth full of hay! Seriously! He was standing there stock still, ears laid back, eyes closed, leg cocked up, and not doing a thing about the alfalfa sticking out of his mouth. I'd call to him, and he'd open his eyes long enough to chew a couple of times, and then he'd go right back to sleep before ever finishing what was in his mouth."

I had to admit I was a little bit tickled by my boy's behavior.

"Well, y'all enjoy the laugh, and I'm going to go see how Mr. Munchy is doing this morning after his all-night snacking binge," I said as I walked down the aisle of Big Barn again quietly laughing. No, he'd never missed a meal—his waistline was a testament to that—and now I knew why.

When I see my heavenly Father, I hope to be waiting with as much diligence as Marquise. He was prepared. With that mouthful of hay, he could tackle a midnight case of the munchies. He wasn't going to be caught hungry, and there was no way his pasture-mate, Sheik, was going to steal the last bit of alfalfa from his possessive incisors. He had everything he needed to make it through the night.

We can take a lesson from Marquise when it comes to the assured return of our Savior. We have to prepare ourselves every minute and not allow our souls to be hungry while we wait for Him.

> But about that day or hour no one knows, not even the angels in heaven, nor the Son, but only the Father.

> Mark 13:32

24

The Equine Triathlete

The eventing horse competes ferociously and without apology in three different disciplines—dressage, cross-country, and stadium jumping. For three days a horse calls upon athleticism, bravery, and suppleness in an equestrian tradition inspired by the art of war. Until I attended the Rolex Kentucky Three Day Event, I never understood the magnitude of each rider's skill or the authority under each saddle.

Each day I watched as Phillip Dutton and Connaught set the bar for the competition.

Day 1: Dressage

My seat seemed a mile high in the gray blustery air as I climbed the metal stands of the Rolex Stadium. Fumbling with my rented commentary headset wasn't making the climb any easier. After stepping on several toes and accidentally bumping a woman on the head with my bag, I settled into my seat.

The packed stadium was oddly silent except for the sound of hooves sweeping gracefully across the sand and the occasional spectator's reaction. After a few moments of confusion, I plugged in the headphones and listened as the voice on the other end gave commentary on each horse and rider. At times she spoke quietly as if at a golf tournament, and at others she punctuated a misstep with an "Oh, dear" or a quiet giggle. Without fail her knowledgeable voice crooned through the tiny electrical wires and into my ears and brought the classical movements of dressage to life.

I'd never studied a trot with such scrutiny or been able to tell whether it was working or collected. Engagement and impulsion became more than words as the long-legged, rhythmical bay propelled himself and his rider the length of the sixty-meter arena and then fluidly through each corner. From the entrance at A to the final halt at X, the being above and the one beneath were synchronized in timing and beauty.

Day 2: Cross Country

I felt a rumble under my feet as a horse and rider burst into view from around a curve in the course. I instantly recognized the source of the rumbling. The horse's coat glowed sepia while his conspicuous white star revealed the identity of the pair I'd watched breathlessly the day before—Connaught and Phillip Dutton.

The pair streaked over the grass, made a tight left-hand turn behind the Rolex clock, and dashed into the infamous duck pond. Mightily the Irish sport horse launched himself out of the water and over the back of the massive wooden duck with inches to his credit. Erupting from the murkiness, the pair stretched upward toward the bank and left the water sulking in defeat.

Day 3: Stadium Jumping

The silence was complete as Connaught entered the Rolex Arena for the final time that weekend. He'd executed an impressive two days of competition, and though the demands on his body had been rigorous, he still surged with the desire to perform. Phillip Dutton, runner-up in the 2007 Rolex, held victory at his fingertips. A clear round would mean a win, but one single mistake would snatch away the victory again.

The team was brilliant.

The horse's liquid coat rippled, and his dark tail danced as he and his rider soared over each of the sixteen obstacles. The white sand was a brilliant contrast to display their perfect movements. One minute and twenty-seven seconds later, Dutton and Connaught claimed the win.

The equivalent of an Ironman Triathlon, the Rolex Kentucky Three Day Event is one of the four most prestigious eventing competitions in the world. The three phases are executed by the same horse and rider team, and the two must excel in all.

A successful horse, like Connaught, must master each critical element: the quiet suppleness of dressage, the athleticism and courage of cross-country, and the technicality and obedience of stadium jumping.

Three distinct capabilities—one singular horse.

Seems impossible, doesn't it?

Not really. God has always embodied this concept through the Trinity. Sometimes understanding three beings existing as one is incomprehensible until we put it into terms our humble minds can grasp.

The eventing horse is one horse that very capably performs in three distinct ways, as does the Trinity. The Father, the Son, and the Holy Spirit are three very different persons of the one true God.

God is the Father almighty and maker of heaven and earth. He is the power above the universe and also our gentle *Abba* when we are in need of comfort and peace.

Jesus is the Son of the Father yet was born of human flesh. It's His birth we celebrate at Christmas and His death we remember at Easter. His time here on earth was a lesson to us in forgiveness, love, and grace, and it's through His death that we can boldly approach the throne of God as righteous heirs to His love.

The Holy Spirit was sent to be a counselor and friend whose presence gives discernment in matters of right and wrong as well as leads toward salvation. Once we seek a relationship with God through faith, the Holy Spirit remains to encourage us along a path of righteousness and dwells with us as we learn to function within the body of Christ.

Though there is no perfect explanation of the Trinity, the eventing horse provides us with a beautiful illustration.

> And I will ask the Father, and he will give you another advocate to help you be with you forever—the Spirit of truth. The world cannot accept him, because it neither sees him nor knows him. But you know him, for he lives with you and will be in you.

> John 14:16-17

25

I'll Never Let Go

A birthday is supposed to be memorable, but not in a way that makes you think it will be your last.

⚜

The forecast promised ideal weather for the kind of mountain ride I usually enjoy alone with Marquise. Quite out of character, I invited three friends to come along for my birthday celebration. As a gift the girls dubbed me the trail master, which meant that I was allowed to choose our route. I spent hours studying the trail map and creating the perfect loop to allow plenty of opportunity to explore.

The big day arrived in splendor, and I drank in the sunshine during my drive to the North Carolina state line. The trees came alive with the truest shade of green as the fog lifted to reveal the morning air. All too soon yet not quick enough, my diesel rolled into the tiny parking area, and I felt Marquise's excitement and approval as he pounded the trailer floor. My friends had just unloaded and were already tacking up to hit the trail. In good spirits the four of us filled the mountain air with friendly chatter.

Armed with homemade maps for everyone, I explained the turn-by-turn directions of our seventeen-mile adventure. The girls were amused that I had taken my job as trail master so seriously, so they honored me with the privilege of assuming the lead spot. As we made our way to the narrow trailhead, no one knew I had stashed a copy of the official park map in my saddlebag—just in case.

The impeccably manicured trail was wide and smooth, a testament to my superb mapping skills. It looked as if forest elves had gone ahead of us the night before, tossing rocks to the side and filling holes so our mounts could stretch their legs and move freely down the path. The trail led us to a shaded creek bed where the horses drank deeply from the crystal water dancing over the rocks underfoot.

So far the day exceeded my expectations. Our horses moved with powerful grace as we climbed up and over a mountain. At the bottom we picked up a floating canter and followed the enticing curves of the trail as it looped around a peaceful lake. Birdsong echoed through the trees and mingled with rhythmic hoofbeats. It became our personal soundtrack for the day. Hindered only by the occasional gravel or technical climb, the horses grew stronger by the mile.

Sadly few good things last forever, and our perfect trail ended abruptly. Looming overhead, the granite rock face mocked our stunned expressions.

"That's the trail?" Daphne asked.

It surprised me as well, so I pulled out my secret copy of the real trail map to make sure we were still on track. The only way to get out of climbing that menace was to go back the way we came. Stuck with what my now questionable mapping skills had dealt us, we decided to forge ahead. One by one the horses climbed through loose rocks and demanded intense work from their muscled hindquarters.

A horse with less heart couldn't and *wouldn't* have made that climb. Luckily our mounts were as committed to us as we were to them. They willingly gave us their all. As I peered down at the conquered rock beneath us, thankfulness surged through me until I saw what was next. The way down was just as treacherous.

Daphne and I chose to walk beside our boys while the braver souls trusted the surefootedness of their mounts more than themselves. Though sheer and technical, the rock was dry, and the horses found secure footing for the descent.

Relieved to reach level ground, I wiped my clammy hands on my tights and tried to suppress nervous laughter. A heavy weight lifted from my shoulders as I settled back into the saddle. The trail welcomed us again.

According to my dubious trail map, up ahead we were to turn right at a break in the trees. My carefree heart stayed afloat only a few moments longer before it sank again. I gasped at the surprise waiting for us—a river.

The four of us stood shoulder-to-shoulder on the bank and sized up the situation. Directly in front of us was a narrow ridge of granite submerged about four inches underwater. That would take us the thirty yards or so to the opposite bank. The crossing itself didn't look so bad, but I worried about the challenges that surrounded it.

Just a few inches to the left of the crossing was the heart of the river. The calm surface and lack of clarity were evidence of its depth. To the right the smooth rocks began a gradual decent. Where the sun kept them dry was relatively safe. Unfortunately plenty of spots were covered by shallow water and ideal for slippery footing.

Our eyes followed the downward rock slope while our ears tuned in to the familiar sound of water crashing over a waterfall. We realized once again that our only options were to continue on or go back the way we came. We really hated climbing that stupid rock face, so the river won our vote with zero enthusiasm.

I knew my water-loving horse wouldn't balk, so after two of my friends successfully made it to the other side, we boldly stepped out while Daphne waited on the bank for her turn. Our first few steps were on dry ground, but as soon as we reached the submerged rocks, I sensed Marquise's uneasiness. The quiet power of the river on our left fueled a rapid current across the tops of the rocks and made it difficult for him to steady himself.

I encouraged him to press on and fixed my gaze on my friends who waited on the opposite bank. Without warning my seat dropped out from under me, and I fell forward against Marquise's neck. His left hind hoof had lost its grip and slipped into the water's darkness. The awkward angle proved impossible for him to overcome. As he lost the battle, his whole hindquarter disappeared beneath the surface.

Marquise desperately scraped at the slick rocks with his front hooves as he fought the river's current. Paralyzed by fear and tortured by hopelessness, I listened to the horror as he slammed into the cruel rocks. The explosions of breath forced from his lungs and bone-chilling grate of hooves against granite painfully echoed in my ears. I couldn't make it stop.

Get off and give him his head, I inwardly screamed and snapped back to reality.

Kicking free from my stirrups, I leaped from the saddle and collapsed onto the unforgiving rocks. It was then that I fully grasped what Marquise faced. Without success I struggled to gain my footing.

In a burst of power, Marquise surged from the river and landed on the rocks beside me. We thrashed about, but the more we fought, the more quickly we slid toward the waterfall.

My friends watched helplessly from the safety of the bank. The birdsong soundtrack faded behind terrified screams, yet no sound escaped my lips.

Holding onto Marquise's reins as he repeatedly crashed into the rocks endangered me. As he slid farther and farther from the safety of the dry bank, he carried me with him, but if he went over that waterfall, he wouldn't be alone. My only thought was *I'll never let go* and no power on earth could make me.

Eternity lapsed before I found a spot dry enough to stand. I turned to Marquise. He'd given up and quietly lay on the river bed, blowing hard, exhausted from his struggle. Still clutching the reins, I desperately looked at my companion who had carried me for years.

"Come on, baby. I've got you."

His eyes locked with mine, and I hoped he believed me. With one final effort, he rose and lunged toward the dry ground.

That night I realized the spiritual truth of the day's events. As much as I love Marquise and wanted to help him, I couldn't. My strength was powerless. In those terrifying moments, I grasped the significance of my salvation. Before I accepted Christ as my Savior, I was caught in a current of worldly sin. Every day it carried me closer to the edge of death and away from the safety of heaven's shore.

Praise God that Jesus intervened on my behalf. He willingly faced the cross and death for my sins, took the reins of my life, and saved me from drowning in my sin. When He faced death for me, He placed my feet on the solid bank of eternal life. Christ did this as an unconditional act of love so that we all can experience a full and abundant life. There is no greater love than this.

> But now, this is what the LORD says—he who created you, Jacob, he who formed you, Israel: "Do not fear, for I have redeemed you; I have summoned you by name; you are mine. When you

pass through the waters, I will be with you; and when you pass through the rivers, they will not sweep over you. When you walk through the fire, you will not be burned; the flames will not set you ablaze. For I am the LORD your God, the Holy One of Israel, your Savior; I give Egypt for your ransom, Cush and Seba in your stead."

Isaiah 43:1-3

26

He Heard Me Call

"You've got to be kidding me." The night had been much too short, and yet another alarm set at four a.m. didn't make me very happy. I pressed the snooze button and flopped back on my favorite peacock-colored feather pillow.

It was one of those spring mornings—the kind where I'd slept with the bedroom window open and let the wind from a midnight storm tickle my cheeks. The clatter of rain on the roof and the distant thunder's low rumble rocked me all night. The bite of the chilled wet air made me scoot deeper under the covers to forget what the alarm wouldn't let me.

After the third, possibly fourth or fifth, time I hit that button, I was officially running late. I began my morning ritual in turbo speed. I threw back the covers and made a dash to the bathroom sink to grab my coffee cup from the day before. I then started the hot water for a shower, tripped over both black dogs in the still-dark bedroom, and let them out the front door. I grabbed a fresh coffee cup from the cupboard, filled it to the brim, and drank a couple of sips while hustling to the porch to scoop cat food into the cat dish. I revisited Mr. Coffee to top off my cup of morning medicine and then hustled back to the steamy shower.

I'm not sure how my teeth got dried and my hair got flossed (or was it the other way around?), but finally I was dressed and able to run down the basement stairs to grab my tennis shoes from the floor of the mud room. With my shoes on, I tucked my freshly filled mug in the crook of my elbow, tightened my belt with one hand, and opened the door of what's known as my horse closet to grab a pocketful of treats.

Twenty-two minutes and counting. It was a record but definitely not one I cared to challenge. Exhausted and stressed-out, I had a mere eighteen minutes to make the sixteen-minute drive to work, but I still had one hundred and twenty seconds to see my boy. *This* was the one thing about being awake before my neighbor's rooster began to crow that made me smile.

I could see Marquise's prone silhouette in the barn's shadows. It was his favorite place to sleep at night. On either side of him, beams from the shedrow security lights gave him a visual safety buffer, and the ever-present Arn stood as his sentinel in the stall doorway. The moment captivated me. For a grand total of five seconds, I was totally unaware of time and space. T minus one hundred and fifteen seconds and counting.

My shrill bobwhite whistle drifted solo through the air until it reached Marquise's ears. They pricked. He knew the sound, and his awakening was much sweeter than mine.

Since the first time he came home with me, I've used this same whistle to call him to me to give him his food, treats, or a good grooming. The morning still weighed heavy in the air, so he knew the call couldn't be a trick to go for a ride. Stretching out his front legs, he graciously rolled to his feet and sauntered toward me.

"I've got to go in ninety-seven seconds. Come on!" I actually heard each second tick by as Marquise walked the excruciatingly long twenty-five yards to the fence and reached out his nose for a treat and a scratch. "I'm flattered you fit me into your schedule this morning, big guy. You can go back to bed now." I breathed a sigh knowing Marquise had survived yet another night out in the wide, wide world, but now I *seriously* had to get to work.

When God calls, I wonder if I hear Him?

He's described so many times as a still small voice—like my bobwhite whistle—that quietly beckons. Sometimes when His call reaches my ears, I hear it and walk toward Him, but when I'm too busy and distracted by life, even a bullhorn can't get through to me.

Marquise has it figured out. His ear is trained to my call, and when he comes to me willingly and quickly, I'm able to reward him. For us an ear trained toward God offers guidance, encouragement, love, hope, and peace—the promise of an eternity of joy and freedom.

We have to look with confidence into the future. He will return for His children, and when He does, will we be distracted by the insignificant, or will we be waiting at the fence for Him? His promise is true. We are His, and one day He will come to take us home.

> My sheep listen to my voice; I know them, and they follow me. I give them eternal life, and they shall never perish; no one will snatch them out of my hand.
>
> **John 10:27-28**

27

The Squeeze

A rainy spring washed the trails clean and brought the grass and foliage to life. Beneath the fallen dead leaves, the gray stones had spent the autumn and winter months hidden by nature's cover and now peeked from under their blanket to enjoy the sunshine.

I was thankful for the boots on Marquise's bare hooves that provided traction as well as protection. My tenderfoot couldn't have tackled those trails without them. As Marquise picked his way through the rocks and muscled us up the mountain with his strong haunches, I wondered how that path had gotten the name Grassy Creek Trail and why it wasn't called "You're Going to Have to Get Off and Walk This One Trail."

Nevertheless we made it to the top and were finally able to pick up a happy trot. The sun's rays, beaming through the treetop canopy, felt fresh and new and made that day's mileage easy and welcoming. We cruised over the worn earthen trails hugging the tight turns like a race car. When brown turned to gray, we slowed but never missed a step, thanks to the additional half inch of hard rubber tread under Marquise's feet. We made quick work of our conditioning ride, and as we looped toward home, Marquise picked up an animated canter. It turned the once warm spring air into a cooling breeze.

We forked off the trail and onto a gravel roadbed that Marquise always loved to stretch out on, but the longer he ran, the more he slowed down. I knew the ride hadn't been enough to tire him, so I asked for more.

"Come on, fella. A few more turns, and we'll be in the homestretch. Can you make it for me?" Marquise surged a little and strengthened for a few extra seconds, but again he sank back. *This isn't normal.* He always gave me his all any time I asked for more. My voice in his ear was all it ever took to bring him to me, but *this* time it didn't work.

"Okay, boy, what's wrong?" I sat back into the saddle and steadied the reins. His eagerness was gone. Frustrated, I reviewed the day's ride hoping to come up with an answer.

What in the world is going on? We haven't gone that hard today. These trails should be a piece of cake to a horse in Marquise's condition. There were no problems coming out of that rocky climb, and he drank like a champ at every creek.

As I went over everything, Marquise's gait slowed even more. He dropped his head asking for a rest, so I hopped off still confused by his actions.

Maybe he's got a rock stuck in his boot, or his tack is pinching somewhere. I began the slow process of deduction, beginning with the saddle and girth. The breast collar had kept the saddle from slipping back, so when I pressed on his lower back, he didn't flinch at all. *This is good. His back's fine.*

I pulled the girth to release the buckles, and the left end swung to the ground. While holding Marquise's reins, I walked to his off side and ran my hand up and down over the smooth, sweaty neoprene still hanging from the saddle. It definitely wasn't the culprit. Thankful I had worn my brown tights that day, I wiped my fingers clean from the sweat and trail dirt before moving on to Marquise's mouth. I checked all sides of his face for rubs, ran my fingers over his gums, and even dropped the bit out of his mouth to make sure he wasn't in pain.

Standing at his head, I caught a glimpse of confusion in his eyes. I could tell he wanted to go on running down the trail but couldn't figure out why he didn't feel so great.

"I know, buddy. I wish you could just tell me what's wrong. I'll keep looking, but if you can manage it, a hint would be great."

I reached down for his front, right foot. Respectfully he lifted it and placed it in my hands. I unfastened the Velcro of the soft fabric that wrapped around his ankle and rubbed my fingers through the soft hair of his pastern. Again nothing. I repeated these steps with the three other ankle straps and cleaned out the tread of each one, hoping to find an unfortunately placed rock. I had no luck, so we slowly walked the last mile back to the trailer.

The saddle felt exceptionally heavy that day as I slid it from Marquise's back. Though the air had cooled, his back didn't even steam. There had been plenty of time to cool down during the walk. Instead of nice patches of damp sweat that rubs off easily, I had clumps of matted dirt and dried salt to brush out. A friend once told me that a good rider never leaves a horse with saddle marks, so I was stuck scrubbing gunk and mulling over a great ride gone bad.

I finished up just as the sun bid its final farewell to the day and its last bit of light collided with the gravel of the parking lot. I leaned over to pull off Marquise's boots and load him up. What I found shocked me. Marquise's heels were as pink as they could be under his wet white hair, and it was obvious when I pressed on them that he was heel sore.

"How stupid am I?" The lot had emptied a few minutes earlier, and I was relieved to be able to have my own verbal tirade without an audience. "I thought of everything and checked everything *except* the absolute most simple. How cruel do you think I must be that I asked you to run all through the woods in shoes that were too small?" I looked Marquise in the eye and wondered if he, in fact, agreed I was stupid. I pulled off the other three boots and sulked at the sight of the strawberry-colored heel bulbs in front of me.

That day I robbed Marquise of his full potential. We had successfully negotiated challenging climbs, cruised over soft trails, and laughed at the rocks, but as the day wore on, the pressure in his feet grew. They became too painful for him to go on. He simply couldn't perform when he was forced into something that didn't fit him.

I bet it's not uncommon for us to do the same. We try to fit ourselves into the world's mold. As we watch the people around us, we desire to fit in and not be labeled as different. Whether it's clothes, houses, cars, or careers, human nature drives us to want to blend in and appear as those around us.

As Christians we have to overcome this mentality. We're called to be different from the world and not squeeze ourselves into its mold. Just as I stole a wonderful trail ride from Marquise and myself, when we try to be of the world, we rob ourselves of the joy that comes from being a child of God.

Do not conform to the pattern of this world, but be transformed by the renewing of your mind. Then you will be able to test and approve what God's will is—his good, pleasing and perfect will.

Romans 12:2

28

It's My Party

"Birthday week" had a ring to it that was far better than "birthday day," except maybe for the one when Mom decorated my cake with miniature Breyer horses. Jeff introduced me to the week-long celebration soon after we started dating, and I was happy to take advantage of his family's tradition when my special day rolled around.

Back then I used birthday week as an excuse for dinner dates, movies, and extra purchases I didn't count as gifts. Now I use birthday week to skip folding laundry, order something for Marquise, and take a day off work to ride.

On that Friday night before my Monday birthday, Jeff and I sat on the couch while he absentmindedly rubbed my feet—my first request of the birthday-week celebration. "So what do you want to do for your birthday? We can start celebrating tomorrow."

"Oh, good. We have the whole weekend, don't we?" I stretched my legs as far as I could toward his thumbs that were squishing the knots out of my arches.

"We do, but let's not go crazy."

"Me?" I asked innocently and tried my best to flutter my eyelashes.

"Yeah, you," Jeff said, grinning. "So what's it going to be?"

"Well, I'd like to ride. Then when I come home, we can trim the hedges together and maybe look at installing that automatic gate opener you got us. After that you can help me hang Marquise's fans in the barn. That'll only take a few minutes and then we can pick up around the shed. You got those steaks, right? You can grill those, and then we can watch a movie."

Jeff's thumbs became temporarily paralyzed. I was sure he was trying to figure out how my birthday week became a reason to make him a slave for the weekend.

"I think you should go ride. You haven't gone out much recently, so I think you'd enjoy that the most. When you get home, I'll have the steaks ready to hit the grill." Jeff was being so thoughtful, and he knew that having a great ride would make the Amber's-best-gifts-of-all-time list. It probably *never* even crossed his mind that if I were gone, his day would be freed up considerably.

"Well maybe." I stood up from the couch, since my foot massage was obviously over, and began puttering around the kitchen to clean up from taco night.

"Riding makes you happy, you know?" Jeff spoke a convincing truth to my heart even though his eyes were still focused on the TV. His recommendation was what I needed more than trimmed hedges and an automatic gate, so after scrubbing the last of the refried beans from a pot, I headed to the study to call Daphne.

The burgundy and brown squares of the area rug were soft on my back as I stretched my newly rubbed feet up in the air and waited to hear my friend's English hello. Once I did, I made the offer. "Hey, you want to ride tomorrow?"

"I've already planned on it. There are a few of us meeting at the North Carolina trails at nine. Do you and Marquise want to join us?"

"Sure, but I haven't been pushing Marquise like I should. If we have to, we can always turn around and come back after an hour or so."

"Sounds good. I know Marquise will be happy to see his old friends."

"You know he will. We'll see you then."

"I'm meeting Daphne at nine," I said as I flopped back into my usual place on the couch and rested my feet back on the pillow in Jeff's lap. "Since you're getting off easy by not having to do birthday chores with me, can you rub my feet?"

Jeff rolled his eyes and reached for a pinky toe.

⁂

Tucked under the quilt my grandmother had made years before, I was wrapped in a cocoon of warmth against the cool morning air that drifted through the open bedroom window. Thunder rumbled through the gray sky and smelled of spring's sweet dampness. Without disturbing the two dogs cuddled against me, I rolled over to see the tip of Marquise's nose sticking out of the barn door and watched raindrops dance in puddles on the driveway.

"Looks like it's going to be a wash," Jeff said as I walked into the living room and headed toward the coffee pot. "I've been watching the weather report, and these storms have stalled right on top of us."

"Great. No riding today." I was totally bummed. There wouldn't be any riding, hedge trimming, gate opener installing, or fan mounting. My whole birthday weekend was shot, and I made sure of it.

I spent Saturday pouting about my missed ride. To make matters worse, my sneaky little dog stole my birthday steak that night. On Sunday we had to be at church extra early, and we spent Sunday afternoon dealing with someone's lost dog. On Monday, although it was finally my birthday day, I griped about everything that didn't go the way I wanted it to over the weekend.

May 20—the worst birthday ever. When Jeff came home that afternoon, I was in the kitchen getting ready to slip on my boots and go tend to the outside animals.

"Have you seen the news?" he asked.

"No. Haven't even had the radio on. Why?"

"They had a tornado in Oklahoma."

"Oh, yeah?" I was still pouting and didn't pay any attention to what he said until he turned on the TV's live coverage and the images filled the room. The devastation was gut-wrenching. Buildings and entire neighborhoods were flattened and unrecognizable. Fires burned while newly homeless people dug through piles of debris in search of friends and loved ones.

The reporter's somber voice recounted the grave facts of the EF5 that had stayed on the ground for forty-five minutes and forever changed lives. "Several farms and racing stables have sustained direct hits, and at this time it's impossible to know how many animals have been killed. It's certain there will be few happy reunions and many heartbreaking realities." The camera turned to a lone horse standing amidst plywood, insulation, and power lines—a grim reminder that animals also suffered physical and emotional pain from the terrible tragedy.

I was at a loss for words and couldn't come up with anything better than, "I'm going to the barn." The creak of the basement stairs that led to the mud room floated past my consciousness and was lost in the echo of the hall. Looking out the window to the peaceful pasture where my red horse stared at the house, waiting on dinner, seemed wrong when a thousand miles away chaos reigned. Guiltily I scooped supplements and wondered about the little girl who'd always wanted a pony and now was without one.

As I watched Marquise and his goats eat, I sank further into my pit, but this time it wasn't because I felt sorry for myself. It was because I was ashamed. I missed a ride because of the rain and a steak dinner because of a little dog. I had let my circumstances change my attitude to one that was self-serving and self-absorbed. Never once during the course of my birthday weekend had I thought about others and how I could be a blessing to them. I had only thought about what I wanted and how I could be served.

The tragedy in Moore, Oklahoma, on my birthday reminded me that it's not all about me. The world didn't stop to celebrate me, but for some people, life did stop.

From now on my birthday week is going to be about more than me. I'm going to challenge myself to do something nice for someone else, make a donation to a cause I feel strongly about, or send a letter to someone I admire. Those things can never be rained out, and they will always change a life.

> Do nothing out of selfish ambition or vain conceit. Rather, in humility value others above yourselves.
>
> Philippians 2:3

29

A Word Spoken in Love

While growing up there were several things I wanted to be—a stork, a tree, and, of course, a horse. As I watched the beads of sweat pop out on the top of Ricky's mostly bald and slightly sunburned head, I was glad that becoming a farrier never crossed my mind.

Every five weeks to the day, Ricky rolls his silver truck into my driveway. Ricky's come to my house every thirty-five days no matter if I've left Marquise barefoot or had him shod. He's adapted well each time Marquise's hoof-care needs have changed. In fact one evening, I called him to discuss a new shoe my vet had recommended, and his exact words were, "I'll do anything up to and including washing dishes to keep that horse of yours sound." Now that's a good farrier. He's punctual, reliable, and just the right mix of knowledge and humility.

That day was no exception. Under the shade of an old sugar maple, Ricky and I spent twenty minutes or so discussing Marquise, how he'd been for the last five weeks, and what the plan was for the next five.

"So how's he been doing?" Ricky asked as he squinted against the bright summer sky and tipped up a half-empty bottle of Gatorade.

"He's good. He seems to be enjoying the heel support from those fancy new shoes you put on last time, but I can't tell you how he's moving. The rain this summer has been ridiculous, so I've barely gotten to ride."

"It sure has, and your pasture is showing it."

"Yeah. Speaking of pastures, I'm going to go get Marquise out of his. I'll be right back."

In a few minutes, Ricky's tools were set up in the driveway under a tiny patch of shade. With a motion that had been repeated a million times before, he wrapped worn leather chaps around his legs and slipped on a pair of gloves as I walked and Marquise waddled toward Ricky.

"Looks like you timed this just about right again, Miss Amber. Those clenches are starting to get loose from all this rain."

"I told you. Five weeks to the day, and we'll be fine. Any more than that, and I'll be calling you to reset a shoe." Ricky and I laughed, knowing good and well that I was right. Two rounds ago we'd tried to go six weeks between shoeing, but on the thirty-seventh day, I was walking my two-acre pasture looking for a thrown shoe. Jeff was mowing every ten days or so to keep the grass under control, and hitting a big piece of steel wouldn't make my grounds-man husband very happy.

The conversation flowed freely with Ricky, just as it always did. We talked about work, the weather, our families, hoof care, mosquito season, and Ricky's cows. It was yet another thing I loved about Ricky—always eager and willing to talk about anything. More often than not, our conversation involved some new hoof trimming, shoeing, or booting trend I'd read about.

We were engaged in a lively discussion about the size of shoes and whether to use aluminum or the steel when my barking dogs alerted us that Jeff was home from work. I knew he'd be joining us soon to get some of the fresh air he craved after a day's work. Sure enough, a few moments later, Jeff walked up behind Marquise and patted him on the rump.

"Hey, Ricky, how're you doing?"

"Good, sir. How about you?" Ricky offered a friendly handshake.

"Just trying to keep this grass down since Amber's horse isn't doing a very good job with it," Jeff said with a wink my way. "If y'all are about done here, I'm going to pull out the mower and start on the upper pasture."

Ricky was already bent over Marquise's front hoof again, calculating which shoe was going to be the compromise, so I answered for him.

"We're done trimming, but Ricky still has to set the shoes. You can go ahead and get the mower out to get started. I'd rather deal with the noise than have to look at this belly on Marquise for much longer. He's a little too fat, so maybe if you scalp the grass, the heat will burn it up, and Marquise's buffet will be a bit more limited"

"Yes, ma'am," Ricky replied.

Ricky was still bent over, so I wasn't quite sure I'd heard him right.

After all, the sound had to travel a long way to make it past Marquise's barrel and up to my ears. "What'd you say?" I asked.

"What?" Ricky asked as he stood up.

"I said, 'What'd you say?'"

"I just agreed."

"With?"

"You."

"About?" This was getting old.

"I just agreed with you about what you said about your horse."

"Huh? That he's a little overweight?"

"Yes, ma'am. A little more than a little." Ricky was kind, but greater than his kindness was his honesty, and he always said he'd tell me the truth. I guess this met his criterion for playing Abe Lincoln.

"Why didn't you say so?"

"Well, over the years I learned to never talk about a woman's weight or her horse's."

"That's actually pretty funny, and most would consider it wise counsel, but I value your opinion, Ricky." I slipped into a very pompous fake accent as I pursed my lips and looked down my nose at him. "You, sir, are an integral part of my horse's healthcare team. I must be able to trust you to give me the truth whether I ask for it or not and especially if it's not what I want to hear." I relaxed my shoulders and returned to my regular ol' country self. "Get it?"

"You mean that?" Ricky's eyes looked straight into mine, and the corner of his mouth turned up in a half smile as he paused for my answer.

"I do."

"Your horse is fat." Ricky spoke the truth quickly, and we both laughed at the elephant in the room that had just been addressed. Unfortunately that day the elephant was a plump chestnut named Marquise.

The truth is a tool we should use to build each other up and to encourage one another in Christ. When Ricky spoke truth to me, it was out of love for me and for my horse. He knew that failure to help open my eyes to the obvious could have led to pain for Marquise and vet bills for me.

As believers we are sometimes afraid to speak truth because we know most people don't want to hear it. Is that a good enough excuse for our silence? Our motivation should be love, and our words should never fail to be a reflection of Christ.

My mouth speaks what is true, for my lips detest wickedness.

Proverbs 8:7

30

Prescribed Burn

It was only the first of July, but South Carolina had already received forty-six inches of rain. The year of the "Great Non-drought" had turned my pasture into a lush oasis and my horse into a chestnut balloon. After Ricky's exhortation about Marquise's waistline, I realized that getting rained out of trail riding every Saturday wasn't helping my boy get the exercise he needed. I was going to have to start making a quick run to my favorite North Carolina mountain trails any opportunity I had—even if it meant going after work during the week and getting home after dark-thirty.

The first day I attempted this, I made great time and was mounted and headed toward the trailhead in an hour and twenty-two minutes. The smell of rain hung heavily in the air, and the gray rolling clouds just above the treetops made me question whether or not the rain would hold off. Settling deeper into the saddle, I squeezed Marquise into a trot toward Buck Forest Road. Ready and eager to respond to my request, I smiled as his hooves clattered rhythmically on the gravel road leading into the woods.

Half an hour of good riding later, I didn't have to wonder anymore if I was going to be able to beat the rain. A crack of thunder split the air, and I grabbed the saddle in anticipation of my mount's reaction. Marquise's rump spun against my outside leg as he tried to decide if it would be worth his energy to bolt. Thankfully he decided against it, and we resolved to enjoy the rain.

The year's abundant rainfall had left its mark on the forest in a good way. The leaves on the trees were thick, the creek was rushing, and vegetation lining the trail was a gorgeous electric green. The overgrown forest maze enticed my sense of adventure, and I counted myself lucky to have my equine companion with me. I couldn't see more than a few feet on either side of the trail, and it disappeared entirely each time it rounded a corner ahead of us.

When the thicket-like maze ended, I pointed Marquise's red nose across a gravel road toward another trail. This one was different. There were no vegetative walls on either side. I could see the zigzagging trail for several hundred yards as it wound between trees and hugged the side of the mountain before it eventually disappeared. The forest floor was practically bare. It looked swept clean of all but a sprinkling of pine needles and a few wilted leaves that were left from the previous fall. The contrast between this trail and the one we'd just left was puzzling until I read the sign:

PRESCRIBED BURN
CONDUCTED APRIL 2010
TO IMPROVE WILDLIFE HABITAT

After I got home from my first very wet weekday conditioning ride, I looked up "prescribed burn." I thought forest fires were bad, so I wondered why one would be prescribed. As I read the glowing laptop screen in front of me, I learned that after studying a location's fire risk and history, the forestry service may recommend a burn to reduce hazardous fuel (and thus decrease larger and hotter fires).

In forestry terms, hazardous fuels can be defined as anything that, when burned, poses a risk to property, recreation, or personal safety and well-being. When hazardous fuels build up, the resulting fire can be extremely hot, damaging, and capable of destroying an entire area. In layman's terms, hazardous fuels are the dry dead organic matter that lies on the forest floor.

In a season of abundance when rainfall is at record levels and temperatures are well below normal for summer months, it's hard to imagine such a tragedy. In reality seasons such as this are the perfect foundation for a destructive fire. As vegetation builds up, so does potential hazardous fuel. All it takes is one season of drought, and everything that was once lush and green becomes dry and dangerous.

This can happen in our hearts as well. During times of abundance and when blessings are at record levels—our jobs are secure, our families are great, and our horses are wonderfully fit—hazardous fuels build. Sometimes this abundance can become so distracting that, even though we think everything is going great, we slip into a spiritual drought.

Maybe we aren't praying like we should or prioritizing our lives in view of the eternal. The fruit and greenery in our lives begins to dry up and wilt away, and before we know it, we're a storehouse for hazardous fuel. With the smallest spark of adversity, we burst into flames—hotter and more damaging than if we had kept our lives clear and our view of Him unobstructed.

After a prescribed burn, a forest can recover stronger and healthier, free from insects and disease and blessed with fresh nourishment for the soil. For these same reasons, God allows us to experience burns—adversity, challenges, and painful situations—to strengthen us and clear out the things that distract us from Him. Just as a forest that has recovered from a fire can regain its beauty from ashes, we can also experience growth and refreshment if we allow our refining to mold us into stronger, more beautiful versions of ourselves.

I will bring that group through the fire and make them pure. I will refine them like silver and purify them like gold. They will call on my name, and I will answer them. I will say, "These are my people," and they will say, "The LORD is our God."

Zechariah 13:9 NLT

31

Decisions, Decisions

I'm an in-control kind of girl. I'm always trying to get one step ahead in the game, and I pride myself in planning out even simple tasks to get the best results.

When packing the trailer for a trip, logic must prevail. It should be easy, but what goes in first is determined by what has to come out first. There's nothing worse than getting to camp and realizing your electric tape corral is packed under your feed, hay, spare rain sheet, and sleeping bag. Jeff wonders why I'm so calculated with everything, but it can't be helped. As a descendant from a long line of engineers, it runs in my blood.

Recently my planning—or lack thereof—got me into a little bit of trouble. I'd noticed my caprine problem child (aka Arn) needed a hoof trim. His toes were long, his heels were low, and dirt had built up under his hoof wall. It was definitely well past time for proper hoof care.

Trim time for the goats isn't quite as enjoyable as unpacking wet tents, sleeping bags, and buckets after a rainy three-day horse camping weekend. Arn becomes two hundred and fifty pounds of pure head-butting monster if I even think about messing with his feet. Effectiveness requires all my reserve strength and skills along with tranquilizers, a dreadfully sharp pair of shears, and a helper's extra body weight. By the time it's all over, I'm lucky if one of us isn't bleeding.

Psyching myself up, I began to plan the next official goat hoof trimming session and hoped that all my prerequisite criteria would be met. First, I checked the weather. Is it too cold? Is it too hot? Is it going to rain? Is it too close to dark?

Second, I considered who would be my helper—the person whose job it would be to hold the angry goat still. Is Jeff busy? Is he in a good enough mood to deal with a big white monster throwing him around? Is my dad in town? He's not quite as strong as Jeff, but his willingness to attempt goat wrangling puts a positive checkmark in his column. What about Erin? Her dad describes her as "scrawny but wiry," which I think is Mississippian for crazy stubborn. They were all excellent prospects, but for obvious reasons, my volunteer pool always shrinks after each trim.

Third, I contemplated the time factor. How much time do I have to drug the goat, wrangle the goat, trim the goat, stop the bleeding on the goat, stop the bleeding on myself, and collapse into an exhausted heap in the place where the now not-so-drugged goat has left to find a patch of clover to nibble (apparently no worse for the wear)?

For an entire month, I weighed all the conditions. Some days I had the helper but not the time. Others, I had the time but not the weather. Days turned into weeks, and my little guy's hooves quickly turned into skis. All of a sudden, I looked at him and wondered why he wasn't crippled because of my poor decision.

Sometimes by *not* making a decision, we're actually making a decision. I chose not to work on Arn's feet until I had the perfect circumstances. By doing that, I left him to waddle around with long toes. He never showed signs of pain, which probably would have jarred me to action, but instead he just went about his daily business of thistle eating.

Every day that I did something other than taking care of his needs, I inadvertently ignored him. Even though the things I was doing weren't bad things, they were wrong when they caused me to overlook the needs of a family member.

In our lives we work hard to maintain the delicate balance of priorities. That balance changes each day. The one thing that should always be at the top of our priority list is Christ and our relationship with Him. I'll be the first one to admit how easy it is to blow off a quick minute alone with Him and His Word in exchange for a quick run to the barn.

I may just plan to throw out some hay and top off Marquise's water, but in the end I pull out the fly spray, detangler, and brushes. What should have taken ten minutes quickly becomes an hour, and by the time I make it back from the barn, my time alone with God is gone.

Don't get me wrong. Taking care of our families and pets is never a bad thing, but when that knocks Christ out of the number one position in our lives, it's time to reevaluate.

> But seek first his kingdom and his righteous, and all these things will be given to you as well.
>
> **Matthew 6:33**

32

Drop the Reins

"Brrrr! Whose idea was this anyway?" I had just stepped from behind the trailer, and the full force of the chilly spring wind smacked me in the face. The tall thick grass beyond the DuPont State Forest parking area swayed in time with gusts that howled through the treetops, and the sunny glow that reflected off the gravel teased me with only pseudo warmth. "I thought it was supposed to be nice today."

"Technically it is. Sixty and sunny is a perfect day for riding, but that wind cuts straight through. Do you need another jacket?" Sheree played the perfect hostess as I shrugged out of my flimsy zip-up and reached for the fleece she offered.

"Thanks." I meant it.

Sheree had supplied me with a horse, a ride, and now a jacket, but *I* was the one who was supposed to be doing *her* a favor. With only four-teen days left to prepare for her first hundred-mile endurance ride, I'd been enlisted as her crew for the day of competition as well as a training part-ner for the pair's last conditioning ride. If I wanted to be worth more than a plugged nickel, I needed to start doing rather than whining, so I picked up a brush to get Bailey saddle ready.

Sheree rescued Bailey when she was only six months old, and the little black filly had grown into a great horse. She was capable of carrying Sher-ee's husband, a beginner rider, and now me.

After a little bit of extra jigging during the windy mounting process, we were finally up and headed toward the woods. Those particular trails were some of my favorites, and the miles I often rode with Marquise tick-led my memory. I loved to sneak away with him on summer evenings to shake off the burdens of real life. A few miles at a good clip never failed to put my mind back where it should be.

Daydreaming about riding Marquise was nice, but at the moment, I had a really good horse under me and a really strong one in front. Sheree had stopped at a fork in the trail and patiently waited on Bailey and me to catch up and decide which way to go.

"Sorry. Left." It was all the guidance Sheree needed from me to kick her long-legged mare back into gear and motor up the steady incline. The cozy fleece and steady exercise along the uphill wooded trail warmed me up. After taking a few more turns, a couple of downhills, and a long canter or two, we arrived at a wide granite-bottomed creek. There, while watching those watery rocks, more memories with Marquise slid into my mind— only these weren't good ones.

The waterfall.

Ever since Marquise and I had barely escaped that fatal fall, even small water crossings scared me. As we approached, I sat deeper in the saddle, effectively slowing Bailey and delaying the inevitable. The memory of Marquise's hooves scraping against the rock haunted me while Sheree's lively chatter drifted past my ears and was lost to the sound of the gurgling creek.

I can't do it. My thoughts didn't form words until Sheree and Riihah were on the opposite bank and turned to look at me.

"I can't do it!" I called to her. Bailey shook her head with disgust and pawed her displeasure about being separated from her pasture mate.

"She's fine. She'll go." Sheree said, thinking Bailey was the one pitching a fit rather than me.

"It's me, not her." Yelling over my shoulder, I turned Bailey away from the creek again. She shook her long black mane and threw her nose up in an attempt to rush the water. Bailey and I were both frustrated, and my fear made the situation worse.

I weighed my options. I could have hopped off and waded across, but the water that rolled by was at least knee deep and icy cold. The rocks were just slippery enough that trying to cross while balancing on them would have ended in a very cold, head-to-toe bath. Turning around would have taken us back to the trailers. There was no other option. It was time to face the water.

"Let her go. She's fine. Just drop the reins and trust her. She'll get you across."

I breathed deep, dropped the reins, and yielded to the leadership of the black horse beneath me.

Cold water drops landed on my legs as the mare's big feet splashed through the water. Bailey confidently waded through the creek toward the other side while I concentrated on simply breathing. Before I knew it, we stepped onto the bank. Rivers of water trickled down Bailey's legs and puddled at her feet.

I trusted Bailey, and she did exactly what was needed to get me across safely.

Whether I'm on the trail or not, fear can get to me—especially when I'm facing big decisions. By nature I want to control things and weigh the pros and cons of each option, but sometimes the answer still isn't clear.

I've learned from years of riding that if the way isn't clear or if the footing is unsure, drop the reins and trust your mount. It's the same with Christ. He's faithful and true and wants to protect us, but unless we drop the reins and allow Him to carry us, we'll always be floundering on the opposite side of His will.

The LORD is good, a refuge in times of trouble. He cares for those who trust in him.

Nahum 1:7

33

Get Out Before the Flood

Sheree and I counted down the few hours that remained before her first hundred-mile endurance ride. We sat outside her trailer in the middle of an outdoor rug and sorted through the contents of her saddle pack to kill time.

"These look yummy. What are they?" I asked holding up a baggie of what looked like jelly beans. "You're going to tell me these are a healthy trail snack, aren't you?"

"Yep. Electrolyte jelly beans. They're keepers."

"What about this?" Pinched between my thumb and forefinger, I dangled what was once a chewy granola bar but was now a hard lump in the end of a foil wrapper. "Whatever it was, it expired last year."

"I'm liable to eat anything if I get lost out there in the dark." Sheree leaned forward, snatched the lump from my hand, and stuffed it deep into her pack.

I laughed. "I told you I'm crewing for you until eleven tomorrow night. I can't stay awake much longer than that, so there's no time for you to be getting lost out there."

"You're so supportive." Sheree's smile held more than a touch of sarcasm. "It's pretty rotten weather for the first week of May, isn't it?"

"Yeah. I expected hot and sunny, not this cold, windy, chance-of-rain mess we're going to end up with." As if on cue, my phone rang. "Hang on a sec. It's Jeff."

Sheree rolled her eyes at my teenage smile.

"Hey, what's up?" I said and rolled mine back at her.

"Nothing much. Just got off work and wanted to give you a call to see what the weather's doing up there."

This was just like Jeff—always up to the minute on sports, news, and weather. "It's just chilly and windy. No rain yet. Is it supposed to start soon?"

"That's why I was calling. You guys are supposed to get some pretty heavy weather up there tomorrow night. Are you close to the river?"

"Right beside it. It's where all the good parking is." The French Broad River flowed right through the Biltmore Estate, beside the vet check, and past our camping spot. Heavy rains from the previous weeks had filled it to the bank and left it threatening to spill over.

"Any chance you'll come home tomorrow night?"

"Nope." I sent a teasing wink my friend's way. "Sheree says there's no way she'll be done before dinner, and we'll stick around for the night to let Riihah rest before driving home."

"Okay, but be careful and watch the river. Don't let it sneak up on you."

"You worry too much, but I will. Love you." I clicked off my phone and turned my attention back to Sheree's preparation.

The next morning arrived quicker than I'd wanted and without a drop of rain. The coat-penetrating cold wind sent Sheree and me back to our bags in search of another layer. As we groomed Riihah, nickers from equine athletes who waited on breakfast filtered through the quiet remnants of night, and heavy clouds shielded the sun's early rays.

An hour later the out timer announced the open trail, and twenty-nine horse-and-rider teams trotted out of camp for the first loop of their hundred-mile adventure. After watching Sheree and Riihah disappear, I turned up the collar on my coveralls and walked back to the trailer to gather the few things that I needed to take to the crew area for Riihah's first pit stop.

After a couple seconds of blankly staring at the empty camp and trying to remember all Sheree had asked me to bring, I pulled out my phone and looked at the list she gave me. "Okay. Blue blanket, feed pan, people snacks, cell phone, GPS, and bottled water. Got it." My arms were full to the point of almost dropping everything, but I was determined to make the walk from the trailer to crew area my last one for a while.

As I neared the sea of buckets, pop-up tents, and hay, I struggled to find our crewing spot. The acre or so that would serve as a pit stop for horses and riders was much more alive than it had been the previous night when we stopped there to unload bags, chairs, and hay. I tried to re-create a mental map from the night before using the only two permanent fixtures I could find—an electric fence and a wooden frame.

The four-strand electric fence, which was about four and a half feet tall, surrounded the crew area on three sides. Its end fencepost was directly on my right. The fourth side was bordered by the French Broad.

About thirty yards in front of me, stood a tall, wooden door frame-shaped structure with plastic sheeting hanging from it. Affectionately known to the equestrians of the Biltmore Center as the "car wash," it was used to walk horses through as a desensitization exercise. I knew we were somewhere between these two landmarks, so using the first as a Y axis and the second as an X, I searched for our stash of pink buckets at the point where they intersected.

There it is, I said to myself when I spotted what would be my home for the next twenty-four hours. As soon as I got there, I dropped everything to the ground and stretched my aching arms.

Horses were in and out all day. They came in hot and got stripped of their tack, cooled, checked by the vet, rested, fed, watered, tacked back up, and sent back out to the trail. The blustery cool from the morning never burned off, and not many riders were able to shed their early morning layers. Instead, it got colder and windier.

Sheree chose to pull Riihah early, but by the end of the night, many riders were still out on the trail. Jeff's predicted storms moved in, and the river rose. Heavy drops of rain battered trailer roofs and blanketed horses all night. As the river began to lap at the edges of its bank, riders and crew packed up their belongings and pulled out before it was too late.

By Monday morning, pictures of the crew area began to circulate online. If I hadn't made my mental map, I wouldn't have been able to find our spot. Just beside the huge frame of the equine car wash, our pit stop sat beneath three feet of water. Fence posts that bordered the crew area were just as telling. Murky brown water stood at the height of the third rope rail. A crew person sitting where I had been two days before would've benefitted from the use of a snorkel.

Any bucket, blanket, or feed pan that had been left there was certainly lost, and anyone who hadn't pulled their trailer out early the day before was stuck on the high ground of the back field for at least another day.

There's something to be said for preparedness. Noah certainly believed in it. We've all heard it said before that it wasn't raining when Noah built the ark. We can use that fact as a lesson that can be applied to many areas of our lives.

It seems obvious in the area of horsemanship. Most of us would never think about tackling an endurance ride, a rodeo, or a dressage test without preparing, so why then is sharing Christ in our daily lives any different?

The Lord will provide opportunities for us to share Him with others, but sometimes we aren't willing because we don't feel prepared. We can overcome that feeling by studying Scripture and committing it to our hearts, so it readily and easily flows from our mouths. We can also live in such a way that Christ is revealed through our actions.

Day by day prepare to be a reflection of Christ and a constant example of His love.

> You are the light to the world. A town built on a hill cannot be hidden. Neither do people light a lamp and put it under a bowl. Instead they put it on its stand, and it gives light to everyone in the house. In the same way, let your light shine before others, that they may see your good deeds and glorify your Father in heaven.
>
> Matthew 5:14-16

34

The Art of Worry

The list of things I worry about goes on and on and dates back to the first night I brought Marquise home. Hours after my bedtime, I tossed back and forth, worrying that his head was stuck in the water bucket. Now what in the world convinced me that an eight-year-old horse forgot how to drink out of a bucket between Bristol, Tennessee, and Greenville, South Carolina, I'll never know. Regardless, I got up at five a.m. and drove to the barn to make sure he was okay.

Next I had Marquise insured—major medical and life insurance. My friends called me crazy, but after the third time I used it, Jeff decided I was the smartest person in the world.

My newest ounce-of-prevention tactic has been to write my phone number in permanent marker on all of Marquise's hooves before a storm. Of course, if you think about it for only a second, you'll realize identification on just one *should* be enough.

If the weather is rotten, I worry about a downed fence after a storm, but when it's nice my overcharged imagination wanders to what would happen if I lost Marquise. What if he dumps me on the trail and runs off? What if we are in an accident on the highway? What if someone following behind us just happens to be pulling a trailer, stops, takes Marquise right out of my trailer, loads him up, and steals him? What if? What if? What if? I can do this for days.

I ride Marquise in a halter-bridle combo with my name and number engraved on a heart-shaped luggage tag, and stuffed in the bottom of my saddle pack is at least one of my business cards. I check my fences once a day, my hitch twice before pulling out, and my girth three times before mounting. During cold snaps Marquise drinks a special water concoction to ward off a belly ache, and in the summer his highness has two giant fans to keep disease-carrying mosquitoes at bay. One can say, without reservation, that I worry too much. In fact, I worry to a fault.

Finding a balance between caution and excessive worry has been tricky, but once God convicted me that my worry was a result of idolizing Marquise, I knew I had to deal with it. For so long I'd been the little girl who had always dreamed of having a pony. When my dream finally looked at me through big brown eyes, I realized that I was scared to death to lose it. I wanted to do everything in my power to keep Marquise safe in order to avoid the pain of ever being without him.

Despite everything I've done to keep Marquise safe and claim him as mine, one thing still remains—God's got this. My worry about the things that may or may not happen will never be greater than the love Christ has for me and that horse grazing in my pasture.

I'm sure that in the future I'll continue to be cautious. I'll continue to double-check gates and sleep with my bedroom window open, but I'll also do my best to remember that my first responsibility as a follower of Christ is to seek Him. When I do this, He'll guide me to care for my horse to the best of my ability today and then give me the strength to deal with the worries of tomorrow.

> Therefore do not worry about tomorrow, for tomorrow will worry about itself. Each day has enough trouble of its own.
>
> Matthew 6:34

35

Diamond M

Many things, including my predisposition to worry, affected my decision to have Marquise freeze branded. I was staking my claim on that cute red-headed attitude and making sure everyone knew that the spunky rotund chestnut belonged to me.

Even though I know Marquise will be mine forever, a brand is permanent and not something to pursue without serious thought. One of my friends had all her horses branded, and they looked great, so I decided to call her for some advice.

"Before you put anything permanent on your horse, you may want to take the extra step to make sure your brand isn't already registered." Her words echoed with experience and wisdom, but they may as well have been Greek.

"Registered?" I hadn't even thought of that.

"Yeah. You send some paperwork in to the state, and your brand officially becomes your property so that everything with that brand can be traced back to you."

"So I design my own brand, send in paperwork, and then have it done?"

"Yep. It's that simple."

A month later, after registering the Diamond M with the state of South Carolina, I called a man who'd been making a living branding almost as long as I'd been alive. It only took a few minutes of talking before I was comfortable enough with his experience and knowledge to hire him.

Traditional branding, as we know from the days of *The Wild Wild West*, has a terrible reputation, and I feared anything that would cause Marquise pain. Even though everything I read claimed freeze branding was relatively painless, I still struggled. For days I weighed the pros and cons, but in the end the pros won.

⁂

The entire morning threatened rain the day Jake was scheduled to show up, but just before our appointment time, the looming clouds broke for the powder-blue sky. Arn and Ole were shooed into the spare stall, locked out of the way, and I'd just started mucking Marquise's stall when my phone rang.

"Ms. Amber, I'm here sitting in your driveway."

What? He's early—way too early.

"Okay, I'll be there in a second. Let me round up the dogs, and I'll meet you at the gate." A twinge of panic tugged at my sanity. The sedative Dormosedan that I'd slipped under Marquise's tongue had yet to take full effect, so I was going to have to kill some time. Lucky for me there's one thing a good Southern girl can do, and that's kill time talking.

I met the big—I mean huge—diesel at the gate and mentally named it "Big Country." This was definitely the kind of vehicle a brander should drive. The enormous white truck had a red-lettered logo across the entire windshield, a Wyoming license tag, and running boards as high as my knees. Behind the cab, a diamond-plate flatbed held about fifty brass branding irons all strapped down tight beneath the shadow of a barrel of liquid nitrogen.

My stomach flinched as Jake started laying everything out. Clippers, buckets, irons. They all played a role in what was about to become a permanent part of my horse's identity. So why did it bother me? Marquise would never belong to anyone else, so putting my brand on him shouldn't matter. Then it hit me—I was worried about what other people might think.

What if people judge me? What if they think I did it without caring about Marquise? What if they think I did it for the look and not for what it was intended? While Jake and I waited on Marquise's sedation to kick in, my thoughts were all over the place like a bull playing Cowboy Pinball. Then he told me this story. Like every cowboy story, it's true.

One night a man's herd of cattle got out of the fence and wandered down the road. Four miles later, the rambling bovines found their way to a nearby ranch. Being neighborly and not wanting harm to come to the animals, the well-meaning rancher opened his gate and let the two herds mingle.

A couple of days later, the sorting began. The two men stood on the top rails of the fence while their hired hands drove the livestock through chutes and into a stock trailer. The man with the lost cattle pointed to each cow that was his, and the cowboys cut them away from the herd, until he came to one.

"That one there with the white ear. That one's mine."

The man beside him was incredulous. "You're crazy. That heifer belongs to me."

"No way. She's getting on that trailer right now and going back down the road where she belongs."

"Well, sir, if that's the way you're going to be about it, they're all mine, every last one of 'em. And those on the trailer—well, they're mine too." The angry rancher demanded that his neighbor leave his land.

Without the ability to prove which cows were his, the man from down the road lost his herd.

It's a pretty dramatic story, but it should give us a reason to ask ourselves what *our* brand looks like. What mark shows in our lives to identify what or who owns us? Is it our job, fashion, money, family...or is it Christ?

I'm branded.

When I surrendered my life to Christ, He marked me for the whole world to see. He did it because He cared enough to claim me. When Christ called me to follow Him, I knew it might hurt a little in the beginning, but as I grow in my faith and relationship with Him, His brand becomes more and more a part of my identity.

When the day finally comes and it's time for me to go home, Christ will scan over the heads of everyone who's mingled together and point to *His* brand and say, "That one there—the one with My mark—that one's Mine."

> From now on, let no one cause me trouble, for I bear on my body the marks of Jesus.

Galatians 6:17

36

The Long Winter

"Boy, you're a nasty mess. I can't wait to get you cleaned up." Marquise dutifully followed behind me through the pasture gate and struck an arrogant pose at the hitching post. I love a clean horse, and he was anything but that. I had my work cut out for me.

The upstate South Carolina winter hadn't been particularly cold or harsh, but we'd seen our fair share of rain. Instead of putting Marquise up on those dreary days, I left the stall gate open on my shedrow barn so Marquise could decide whether he wanted to be in or out. I might be cold, wet, and chilled to the bone, but he'd choose to stand in the drizzle and graze happily. The rain tracks down his back and red mud caked around his ankles were a contradiction to the copper shine that normally graced my pasture.

"You're a far cry from looking anything like Hollywood today, aren't you," I told him with a laugh as I ran the shedding blade over his barrel that was perfectly proportioned for a horse twice his size. The blade scratched across the red fuzz on his back and created balls of fur the size of small hamsters. Each time the spring wind blew, the lifeless Marquise-colored critters scampered over the toes of my boots or skipped across the clover. I studied where the shedding blade had been and where it had yet to work, knowing I wasn't even partially done with the task at hand.

Old dry hair lay in sheets across the top of Marquise's coat waiting for the wind or my blade to whisk it away, and though I was doing my best to clean him up, my efforts were in vain. Marquise's thick red tail, that usually sparkled and touched the ground by an inch or more, was greasy, matted with hay, and accessorized with tiny sticks and grass.

If he was going for the Fabio look, his signature golden forelock and mane weren't helping. In lieu of the surgical length clip, which usually ran down the first six inches of his neck, lay a pseudo mane that flopped haphazardly with every step. It was barely long enough to brush but plenty long enough to collect dirt when he rolled every night after dinner.

After the long winter, I was now standing in front of Marquise while he stared back at me with red dirt caked over his left eye and a forelock pointing five different directions. With dirty fingernails that looked like black half-moons, I held a brush full of red hair in one hand and a dirty curry in the other and admitted I was in over my head.

Marquise was filthy with the deep kind of dirt that can't be fixed with a good brushing or a wet towel. Months of buildup had collected against his skin since his last bath, and the only thing able to fix the problem was going to be some good ol' soap and water.

I officially decided the day horses hated above all others had come—spring bath day. He sure needed it to get back to looking like the Hollywood we all knew and loved.

I've been like Marquise on occasion. There have been days—more like months—when I've felt dirty. During my life's wintry seasons, I've collected dirt and become a not-very-pretty version of myself. This could have happened because my actions were out of God's will and pulled me away from Him, or maybe it happened because I just didn't spend time with Him and drifted. No matter what caused my winter, I needed spring and a good bath.

One thing that's super dependable about a relationship with Christ is, just like Marquise's bath, coming back to Him always gets you deep-down clean. God doesn't work superficially. If you'll let Him, He'll get to the really dirty spots and clean them up. He'll give you the strength to search your heart and the wisdom to make life changes.

No matter what caused your winter or dark time when you've felt a million miles away from Christ, He has the power to shine you up and get you back to feeling like Hollywood again.

> Have mercy on me, O God, according to your unfailing love;
> according to your great compassion blot out my transgressions.
> Wash away all my iniquity and cleanse me from my sin.
>
> Psalm 51:1-2

37

Fire Insurance

At an endurance ride campsite, there can be more than two hundred horses, at least that many people, and mass quantities of hay. One chilly spring evening the unimaginable happened—fire.

A space heater malfunctioned, exploded, and destroyed the living quarters of a horse trailer. The combustibles inside burst into flames, but the steel front wall saved the propane tank from escalating the tragedy from unfortunate to deadly.

I stared at the images on my computer screen and shuddered. This was reality. Far more than any statistics, those photos were real warnings about the dangers of barn fires, frayed wires, and spontaneous combustion of green hay. This was an accident that could have happened to anyone and easily claimed the lives of horse, rider, and anyone else in the area.

As cautious as I was and as often as I made up stuff to worry about, I didn't own a fire extinguisher—not for my trailer, my kitchen, or my barn. I left fire safety to the good Lord and effectively buried my head in the it's-not-going-to-happen-to-me sand. Admitting my ignorance and reality-denying bliss, I drove to my nearest home-improvement store in search of a trailer fire extinguisher.

This was officially the first day I'd ever stood motionless in a home-improvement store staring at products on a shelf. While I grappled with A, B, and C ratings, no little man in a vest miraculously appeared to clear things up for me. I was on my own.

After weighing my options, I settled on the new model of a traditional unit. According to the label, its discharge rate was four times longer, covered a surface area three times greater, and was easier to use. Looking like a stylish can of hairspray, it was sized comfortably for the palm of my hand,

and I already knew what pocket it would fit in my trailer door organizer. For the low price $29.99 plus tax, I purchased peace of mind.

⁂

Theresa and I arrived late at camp for the Mountin' Hopes Endurance Ride, which was held on the grounds of the beautiful historic Biltmore Estate. Theresa's sister held a campsite for us in the overflow parking and had already set up our corrals, since she knew we were going to be pushing to arrive at a decent time.

I was thankful for her consideration when we pulled in after ten p.m. and soon realized that making camp in the dark wasn't easy. Buckets were dark, fences were dark, and the horses were dark. It was so dark that even the moon was dark. An owl's hoot echoed through the nearby woods—probably calling for a friend he couldn't see because it was so dark.

Sooner than usual we called it a night and agreed to share breakfast cooking duties in the morning. Wearily I curled up in the gooseneck of Theresa's trailer, made her promise not to make fun of me when I started talking in my sleep, and drifted into the comforting dream zone filled with open pastures and nickering horses.

"Fire!" Theresa's panicked scream woke me with a jolt. "There's been an explosion by the vet check. Get your fire extinguisher now!"

My feet hit the floor before she'd gotten the full sentence out, and she followed close on my heels as I ran through the wet grass toward my trailer. *Where is it? Where is it?*

My new emergency equipment had taken up residence in my trailer only two days before, and I'd just thrown it in instead of putting it in the chosen organizer pocket. Supplies from setting up camp were strewn all over the floor of my dressing room. Cold beads of sweat popped out on my forehead as I fumbled through the darkness.

"Here it is!" I grabbed the canister, ripped the top off, and ran toward Theresa. "Where's the fire?" I looked in the direction her finger pointed, out across the sea of horses, hay, and trailers.

A gasp caught in my throat. Towering flames licked the sky, and in its shadow, I saw the outline of a panicked horse circling its corral. "Come on!" My thoughts narrowed on the people who still slept and the horses that could possibly be trapped if the fire turned into a deadly explosion.

I ran straight toward the orange and red blaze, clutching what I believed was the canister of life, and Theresa was hot on my heels.

"Left! Left! Left!" Theresa screamed at me, hoping to avoid another disaster. I quickly changed course and barely avoided impact with a wire fence. The rapid change of direction and the long wet grass under my bare feet brought me down in a full-fledged face plant. My pink polka-dot pajamas immediately soaked straight through, and the nighttime dew numbed my toes. I pushed myself up and ran forward again.

As I neared the fire, my breath came in short gasps due to my lack of any regular physical fitness routine. Adrenaline urged me on as I accepted my role as rescuer. Theresa's footsteps no longer echoed behind me, and with a quick glance over my shoulder, I saw that she had slowed to a walk. *Saving this place is up to me! I have to get to the fire!*

Nauseous from lactic acid and my lungs' lack of oxygen, the ninety seconds that had elapsed between Theresa's scream and my last step seemed to have taken an eternity. Faces surrounding the flames stared at me.

"Take the fire extinguisher." I offered the can from my left hand while I bent over and supported my breathless frame with my right. Exhaustion had won. Was there no one else willing to fight the flames with me? Why was there no panic, and why didn't anyone take the can?

"Take it! I know it looks like hairspray, but please take it!" I couldn't get anymore words out, but now that my feet were stopped, the world came into focus.

"Girl, I think they've got this one." I hadn't even noticed Theresa slip in behind me. Her hand rested between my heaving shoulder blades.

"What?" My questioning eyes met hers, and then I looked from one face to another. It all looked so organized, so…planned. The man beside me held a propane tank with a hose attachment—I assumed some kind of flame thrower—and beside him was a woman with a bucket. Two more men stared at me like I was a raving lunatic.

"What?" I asked again, not able to make sense of it all.

"You didn't notice the barrels?"

I did after she said this. Two fifty-gallon drums were stacked with holes cut in the bottom for air flow. This fire was intentional. But why?

"It's the pig pickin' fire. We didn't notice it when we drove in, and I never thought they'd be starting it in the middle of the night."

The faces reflecting the red glow of the fire confirmed it. I'd been had and would soon be the butt of a lot of jokes that involved pink polka-dot pajamas and a palm-sized fire extinguisher.

What looked like a can of hairspray to others, in my mind was the sole way to save camp. During my desperate run through the wet grass and almost through a fence, I clung to the hope that my fire extinguisher would save lives.

In so many ways we can view our relationship with Christ the same way—as fire insurance. We want to have it just in case but don't think twice about leaving it buried under a bunch of junk while we get on to more important things. When there's no emergency and the heat isn't on, it sits on a shelf, and we proclaim to the world that we're Christians. Don't we look good—all nice and trendy as the new model of the old traditional!

That's not the kind of relationship Christ wants with us. He doesn't want to be our fire insurance but rather our fire prevention. Walking with Him each and every day improves our attitude toward life, strengthens our ability to withstand crises, and helps us handle everything with less worry and more peace.

So don't wait for an emergency. Seek God today and tomorrow go ahead and pack that fire extinguisher in your trailer…just in case.

> For no one can lay any foundation other than the one already laid, which is Jesus Christ. If anyone builds on this foundation using gold, silver, costly stones, wood, hay or straw, their work will be shown for what it is, because the Day will bring it to light. It will be revealed with fire, and the fire will test the quality of each person's work. If what has been built survives, the builder will receive a reward. If it is burned up, the builder will suffer loss but yet will be saved—even though only as one escaping through the flames.

1 Corinthians 3:11-15

38

My Favorite Hay Bag

When Marquise got hurt last fall, the vet uttered those dreaded words—
stall rest. He may as well have told me to move the moon, because like
many of you know, a stall is to many horses anything but rest.

Marquise is one of those horses. He's been on full pasture ever since
I've owned him, and though he came from life in a stall, he's gotten quite
accustomed to having access to a full-time buffet.

A winter without exercise and grass made the possibility of develop-
ing colic a very realistic concern, so as his person/caretaker/torturer (as he
thinks of me during stall rest), I began the search for the perfect hay bag. I
needed a way to provide him with plenty of roughage at a slow pace, and
I had to figure out how to get extra water in him. That wasn't too much
to ask for, was it?

Luckily I came across this fantastic idea in an online catalog—a slow-
feed hay bag with small two-inch diameter holes and a large, easy-fill top
opening. As I studied the design, I figured out a way to slow Marquise's
eating and get him the extra water he needed all at the same time. If I
filled the hay bag and closed the top securely with a couple of snap hooks,
I could then drop the bag into a tub of water to soak while I did my barn
chores. After about twenty minutes, I could pull it out and hang it in Marquise's stall so he could pick at it until his little heart was content. This was
brilliant and would do the trick if Marquise didn't go mad while trying to
pull the hay out one piece at a time.

The first couple of days didn't go so great. Even though I had my system, Marquise also had his, and he barely touched the bag full of drenched
hay. Obviously he didn't appreciate the wet, drippy mess in his stall, and
since the goats were still allowed to slip under the stall guard, coming and

going as they pleased, Marquise spent the majority of each day pouting and watching them nibble clover from his favorite spot. After a couple days of throwing out waterlogged hay, I called the vet. He shared my concerns about trying to get the extra water in him.

"Marquise hates the wet hay," I said. "Each morning and afternoon, I'm throwing out more hay than he's eating."

"Are you using fresh hay?"

"Of course."

"Fresh water?"

"Every time."

"Well then I guess he's just going to have to get over himself. It might not be his favorite, but as long as everything is fresh and there's nothing wrong with what you're giving him, just stick with it. I've never seen a horse starve to death with hay sitting in front of him."

The vet made a very valid point. Two days later Marquise's bag was empty when I went to the barn, and he was nickering for more. That bag bought me the time I needed between feedings by slowing him down, but it also got the water in him that was necessary to help ward off the dreaded cold-weather colic.

My greatest concern that winter wasn't that Marquise would go crazy from boredom, but that his body wouldn't get the water it needed. Water is vital for our bodies—both humans and horses—to function well. Dehydration, electrolyte imbalance, and—my greatest fear—colic are all very real.

Our need for spiritual water is just as critical, and whether we realize it or not, our bodies and minds yearn for it and find refreshment in it. Just as we would never deprive ourselves or our animals of water, we shouldn't deprive our souls from Christ's nourishment that provides life for eternity.

> Whoever drinks of the water I give them will never thirst. Indeed, the water I give them will become in them a spring of water welling up to eternal life.

John 4:14

39

Stall Rest

Surviving stall rest is an art, not an act. It's not as simple as throwing a horse in a stall, dropping in some hay every now and then, and checking water once a day. At least for Prince Marquise it isn't.

My number-one priority was to prepare his environment. This meant creating an area where he could be happy, healthy, and above all safe.

First I removed the stall gate. His shedrow barn opens directly to the pasture and provides excellent ventilation and air flow while also allowing him to feel less confined. The gate to the stall was a traditional metal mesh, so even though Marquise could see through it easily, he would become very agitated when it was in place.

After some thought and of course some worry, I installed a stall guard. Using six, three-and-a-half-inch eye hooks screwed into the door frame, I situated the guard so it was high enough that he couldn't give jumping it any serious thought and low enough that going under was out of the question.

Once the guard was in place, he immediately calmed down. Problem number one, claustrophobia, solved. Arn and Ole could move freely in and out of the stall, which helped provide physical contact but allowed them to leave any time Marquise felt grumpy.

Toys helped Marquise pass the time. His favorites were an old rubber feed bucket and lead ropes with the snaps removed. I often found them either buried in the sawdust, outside the stall in the grass, or even in the rafters. He would use them to chew, swing, and on occasion smack himself on the rump. Marquise is a very playful, mouthy horse, so anything he could chew on was fair game. This led me to my next task—chew-proof the stall.

If given a chance, Marquise will chew on anything that doesn't have legs to flee, so I made some physical adjustments. Because I couldn't hang up his water bucket for fear of him chewing the edges and enjoying the fun of spilling water all over the stall, I used a muck bucket on the floor.

He chewed the edges of his stall window, so I screwed a one-by-four into its frame about halfway up. This kept him from being able to grab the new board or get a grip on the windowsill. In case you haven't noticed, I am trying to deny that on occasion Marquise will crib. I prefer the term "wood-chewer." Yes, he even tried to chew the stall guard before I soaked it with a bitter spray.

It took me a little while to figure out the bedding. At first I used shavings, thinking they would be softer and less dusty, but I tossed out massive amounts every time I mucked the stall. I finally made the switch to pine pellets. They absolutely carry more dust, but with the fresh air flow from the open stall, I didn't have to worry too much. Marquise was very kind to me and kept an extremely tidy stall. He only peed in one place, and his manure was always piled up nicely in another. I picked his stall twice a day to help keep his hooves healthy and was rewarded with a cleaning task that took no more than three minutes. Yes, I realize I'm lucky.

Finally but most importantly, I carefully inspected every bit of the stall that would be Marquise's new home for a few months. I looked for loose or exposed nails, rotten or wiggly boards, gaps that could trap a hoof, and anything else that could pose a hazard. In the end I had to concede that horses are extremely talented and are bent on challenging the human imagination. They will look for even the most innocent-looking board, window, bucket, or hole and find a way to injure themselves on it.

I had to be creative when I was trying to horse-proof the stall, but I also had to remember that I'm capable of doing only so much to protect Marquise. Even though I knew putting him up in a stall was hard on him for the short term, it was necessary for his long-term healing and soundness.

Sometimes God does the same for us. Sometimes He allows us to be in situations that we may not have chosen or make us uncomfortable. He knows we need them for our continued growth. He has our best interest in the very center of His heart, and He knows our temporary discomfort can often have very beautiful and successful results.

> And the God of all grace, who called you to his eternal glory in Christ, after you have suffered a little while, will himself restore you and make you strong, firm and steadfast.
>
> 1 Peter 5:10

40

The Last Chapter

My mouth will speak in praise of the LORD.
Let every creature praise his holy name
for ever and ever.

PSALM 145:21

Marquise and I had been battling on-and-off lameness for three months, and it was the worst kind—the kind that never quite goes away. After diligent rest with no improvement, I decided a full veterinary workup was in order. X-rays and ultrasound identified a small tear in a coffin joint ligament on his left front, and we accepted our sentence of six to nine months of rest.

We were patient, and six months after his diagnosis, Marquise was running around the pasture just for the fun of it. Despite his soundness, I still wasn't ready to commit to any saddle time. I had the feeling it'd be better to wait the full nine months rather than possibly have to deal with it again in a year or two. So I waited.

When Erin called me at work, it was February, the seven-month mark. "Marquise's lame," she said.

"How lame?" I asked, concerned but not panicked.

"Like three-legged lame. He was laying down when I got here, and when I went out to check on him, he got up but wasn't interested in going anywhere. I went to get the halter to bring him in, and when I came back out, he ran off. Right now I'm cold hosing him, but he's pretty uncomfortable."

"Okay. I'll be there in a few minutes." I was disheartened and didn't understand why this was happening. How could we have come so far only to be let down?

By the time I got home, Erin had Marquise resting in his stall. I stepped in beside him and scratched his favorite spot behind the ear. "Why do you have to be like this, huh, boy? I thought we were done with lameness and ready to get back to work."

His jaws were busy with a mouthful of hay, and his eyelids drooped. I got the impression that he was content and not overly fond of going back to work. Marquise certainly didn't give off the vibes of a distressed horse. Had Erin overreacted?

I left the stall and went to the tack room for a halter. I had to see this for myself. After tying the soft rope at his cheek, I opened the stall guard, and Marquise calmly followed me into the pasture.

We walked a few steps. *Looking good. I'm not sure what Erin was seeing.*

"Trot!" I chirped. Our endurance vet check training came in handy, and he readily stepped out to pick up a trot. For a moment everything was fine, but in an instant, the nonexistent steel jaws of an animal trap snapped shut on his left front leg, crippling his beautiful extended stride. Just as Erin had said, he was three-legged lame.

"Wow." I couldn't believe it. How did a horse go from *that* content in a stall and *that* sound at a walk to *that* lame in a matter of steps? I didn't know, but he was going back into the stall, and I was calling the vet.

Dr. Bryant came out a couple of days later. For years I'd trusted his ability, and in return he didn't even crack a smile when I tried to convince him a yellow-jacket sting was actually a worm erupting from my horse's hide.

From inside Marquise's stall, I heard the rumble of Dr. Bryant's dust-colored diesel as it idled outside my gate. "Hang on. I'm coming," I called as I jogged up the drive.

Sometimes I tend to overreact. I'm sure he expected to see a lameness that was a little less dramatic than what I'd described over the phone, but Marquise obliged and limped pitifully. After an exam, a nerve block, and some flexion tests, we decided I would be better served to rest him until I could get to the local equine hospital for further diagnostics.

A week later Erin rode with me to Tryon Equine Hospital and tried her best to direct the conversation to encouraging things—a new song on the radio she'd heard, a great new brand of jeans she thought would look good with my new cowboy boots, and of course, the weather. I didn't care about any of it. My thoughts were flooded with images of crippled horses and empty trailers, so I braced for the worst.

When we arrived, Dr. Metcalf was a little behind with the previous appointment, so we hung out at the trailer with the patient. I stared at the gravel as I propped myself up against the wheel well and tried to get comfortable. Lost in my worry, I twisted a single piece of hay until it crumbled in my fingers and drifted off in the wind.

Finally the vet techs began to walk toward us. Silhouetted against the sky, they looked like Wyatt Earp and his gang at the O.K. Corral. It wasn't until I unloaded Marquise and his hooves began to crunch across the gravel that I saw something that had been missed when I loaded him. Actually it was what I *didn't* see that surprised me.

Dr. Metcalf met us at the door and directed us back out to a grassy spot. "Go ahead and trot him out before we go inside," he instructed one of the techs.

She took Marquise's lead and proceeded to trot my very sound horse forty yards out and forty yards back. I caught Dr. Metcalf's eye as he gave me a sideways glance. "Um, I didn't see anything. Did you?" He was asking me so he could keep himself from saying, "Did you *really* just drive an hour up here to have me watch a sound horse trot?"

I was sheepish. "I didn't see anything, but I can promise you he was dead lame."

"Really! He was. I'm the one who first saw it," Erin chimed in as my backup.

Dr. Metcalf gave me the benefit of the doubt. "Okay, let's circle him on the firm ground."

Sound again.

"Will you take him in the arena, so we can see how he moves in the sand?" Dr. Metcalf asked the tech. He was doing everything he could to make my horse lame, and my horse was doing everything he could to make me look stupid.

"He's not showing me anything today. You said it was his left front?"

"It was. Do you think it could have been a stone bruise?" I was embarrassed I hadn't even considered that before.

"It could be, but let's do some flexions first, and then we'll take him in and put the hoof testers on him."

Dr. Metcalf flexed all of Marquise's joints, and just as you would expect from a very noncompliant patient, Marquise trotted sound after each one. I was so frustrated, but at the same time relieved that what Erin and I'd seen could have been just a bruise.

The open air inside the hospital was heavy with the smell of hay and speckled with friendly whinnies from equine inpatients. Marquise occasionally answered them with his deep baritone but otherwise stood patiently while Dr. Metcalf's metal testers appraised each hoof. There were no answers. "I agree with Dr. Bryant that we should go ahead and shoot some films and do an ultrasound. Other than that, the best I can do is tell you to haul back up here as soon as you can the next time he's lame."

I'd had X-rays done months ago and really didn't want to spend any more money than I had to. After all, I couldn't imagine trying to explain to Jeff why I was repeating X-rays on a very sound horse, and so I passed.

We walked across the gravel drive back to the trailer, and I patted Marquise's shoulder. "This is going to cost me, you know that, buddy?" Oblivious to what had just happened, he loaded onto the trailer and pulled a mouthful of hay from the net. I picked up my checkbook from the front seat of the truck and went to the office to pay my bill. After all, Dr. Metcalf had done the exam part. Marquise just hadn't done the lameness part.

When we got home, I promptly kicked Marquise out of the stall and into the pasture with the goats where he belonged. All was well—at least for another week.

Erin was at the barn and had to call me at work again. "Marquise's lame."

"Are you kidding me right now? Just put him up, and I'll check him when I get off." No way was I going to hit the panic button again.

This time, rather than following the doctor's orders and scooting up to Tryon, I decided to let it play out for a couple of days. Stone bruises sounded like the obvious answer, and I wasn't putting anything past him.

Another cautious month in the pasture dragged by, and Marquise returned to his normal perfect self. He moved better than he had in years, and I was ready for a day out on the trail. Optimistically I planned a ride with Daphne and Erin for the following Saturday. On Friday while I locked down the hitch of the trailer, Erin's dusty-blond curls appeared from around the tailgate. "Hey, girl, I just wanted to check in before the big day. Are you excited?"

"Crazy excited." The hitch stand rolled up as I leaned into the crank.

"Well, it's looking like I'm not going to be able to join you guys in the morning, but I'm really glad you're getting out. You and Marquise both need it. Do you want to trot him for me one more time? I'll let you know if I see anything."

Trot him? I've only been doing this every two weeks for the last ten months.

"Sure," I answered and went to grab Marquise from the pasture. Once we got to the driveway, I steeled myself for the worst, looked toward her, and clucked to Marquise. "Trot!"

Smooth as silk he floated above the driveway looking like his feet never touched the asphalt. If it hadn't been for the heavy cadence behind me, I would have sworn they didn't.

"Looking good." Erin's eyes sparkled with the happiness she felt for me. "Now it'd be great if you could get back to the trail and get some weight off him before he gives birth."

"Will do," I said, laughing. "I know at least one of us is looking forward to it." My fingers found the all too familiar spot behind Marquise's ear and dug in for a good scratch.

June 4

I couldn't sleep last night. It's been almost a year since my last ride. I was jittery but calm, knowing I needed this time with my best friend. It made me want to cry while I drove up the mountain toward our favorite trail.

It's been hot, but this morning Marquise and I got a reprieve, and God let us enjoy a cool sixty-six degrees. Instead of turning up the radio, I turned it off and prayed something that went like this: Dear Lord, thank You for blessing me with the beauty of this day. Thank You for giving me more than I could ever deserve. You've provided me a good job, a loving family, and today a healthy horse. It's easy for me to praise You on a day like today, but when all this is gone, I pray that You will give me the strength to continue to lift up Your name. Amen.

Daphne and Eclipse met us at the trailhead, and Marquise was excited about seeing his old buddy. I almost forgot how to tack up and probably spent the greater part of five minutes just trying to get my saddle pad straight. Marquise was a booger, and I had to get Daphne to hold him—after all it had been a long time for both of us. I stepped into the stirrup and swung my leg up and over Marquise's back.

Everything about him—about us—felt right. Marquise is like my favorite pair of jeans. No matter how long I leave them folded on the shelf in the closet, everything about them is perfect the second I slip them on.

The first few minutes were rough. Marquise attempted a bit of spirited she-nanigans. He couldn't get his big butt off the ground, and I couldn't find my seat to save my life. All I could think about was my brother trying to teach me how to ride a pogo stick. It just didn't work. When Daphne and Eclipse joined us, everything calmed down, and Marquise settled into a nice calm walk.

My favorite thing about riding a horse I trust completely is being able to lean back and scratch their rump while we're walking down the trail. I bet it feels good to have fingernails get the itchy spots, especially on days when the deer flies are out. Today was no different. I let the reins hang and leaned back on my hand on Marquise's hindquarters. His rhythm was even and comfort-able. I closed my eyes.

Then I felt it. There was no misstep. There was no stumble. In my mind all I could hear was the snap of steel jaws slamming shut.

Marquise was lame again. I could barely steady my voice enough to get Daphne's attention. When she stopped, I held my eyes open wide and willed myself not to blink. I wanted to run back to the trailer so I wouldn't break down in front of her, but my horse was crippled again. We were done.

My heart broke when my feet hit the ground. This was way worse than get-ting a hole in my favorite jeans.

If this was going to be our last walk back to the trailer, I wanted to make it a special one—one that I wouldn't soon forget. We stopped at the creek, and I let Marquise play in the water. No one was around, so I sobbed. It hurt. It hurt to see the joy he got from being that obnoxious water horse.

God, I promise I'll always let him play in the water. Please, please don't take him away from me.

The trailer was in sight, but in front of it was a patch of wildflowers. I stopped and stuck their tiny stems in his bridle. Yellow and white petals looked too happy for today. I wanted to pull them back out and grind their happiness under the heel of my boot. Instead I left them and took advantage of the per-fect afternoon light to take some beautiful pictures of what may very well have been our last trail ride.

I had wanted that day to be a new beginning, and God answered me in a way I didn't expect. I'd hoped for a seamless return to the trail and fellowship at endurance ride camps, but God wanted something else. I can only believe He had plans for something more.

Today I have to face the reality of our last chapter. Though it's the last one on the trail, it's not the last chapter of my life or Marquise's. With hope I turn the page in our story, because I know the only way to begin a new chapter is to end one.

> "For I know the plans I have for you," declares the LORD, "plans to prosper you and not to harm you, plans to give you hope and a future."
>
> Jeremiah 29:11

41

The Sequel

Two days after that ride, I sat on my back porch feeling numb. As I breathed in the smell of my neighbor's fresh-cut grass, I watched drops of condensation form on my water glass and race to the table. Void of anything useful, my mind drifted to the life cycle of sweat on the side of a glass.

Seeming to form from nothing, it first appears as an even sheen and then slowly separates into tiny droplets. The drops grow, and once they're heavy enough, they succumb to gravity and slide down to either be absorbed into a coaster stone or leave their mark as a ring on a fine piece of heirloom furniture. My idle hands lifted my glass and set it down, making rings and joining them together in a bad imitation of what you'd see at the Olympics.

I'm sure the birds were taking part in their usual afternoon activities, hopping through the limbs of their favorite tree that shaded me from the sun, but my mind was blank. My heart felt nothing, only emptiness. I always cheered for the underdog, the one with no hope, a disadvantage, and a strong lack of support, which is why I had to do something other than simply retire Marquise as an underdog. I needed to know why.

I trusted God but still didn't understand. Even though I didn't want to give up my riding buddy, I *could* if that's what God was asking. I hoped for one last shot at understanding why. The only diagnostic test left after the X-rays, ultrasounds, and flexions from ten months prior was an MRI. It was the gold standard of diagnostics and a five-hour haul from home.

A week later I'd scheduled an appointment at Rood and Riddle Equine Hospital in Lexington, Kentucky and was trying to convince Erin to head out on a road trip with me. "I know, Erin. It's a long shot, but if I'm going to give Marquise up, I have to know why." Sitting at my desk in my home office, I drummed a pen with one hand, chewed the nail of my index finger on the other, and held my phone between ear and shoulder while I listened to her.

"You know I'll do anything for you, and if it means taking a road trip, I'm all in, but I just hope you're willing to hear what the vet has to say. You'll get all the answers you need, but they aren't going to magically heal Marquise."

"Yeah, I know," I said trying to maintain a sliver of hope while steeling myself for the truth.

The following Sunday we were on the road headed north with a cooler full of food in the bed of the truck and a bag full of travel snacks in the cab. The trip was easy, and Marquise hauled like a champ, arriving bright and alert as we drove onto the grounds of the twenty-three-acre surgical and wellness hospital.

"Wow! Can you believe this place?" I asked and drove toward the sign for the admitting offices. My open window let in the mid-June heat waves. The late afternoon air was lightly peppered with the sweet smell of horses. "This is the first stop. I'll check us in and find out where we go from here."

It took only a couple of minutes to be greeted by the friendly staff, get my barn assignment, and hop back in the truck. "We're headed to barn five."

"Barn five? They have *five* barns here?"

"You mean nine?"

"Girl, you're going to get some answers here. If not here, then nowhere. You'll just have to ask Jesus when you see Him." Erin's lighthearted teasing made me feel better. I was much closer to the answers I'd needed for so long.

Promptly at eight the next morning, we walked into the client lounge, claimed a couple of tables and a Wi-Fi password, and got down to the business of accomplishing absolutely nothing. Distracting horses were everywhere, and our window faced straight out to the lameness exam area. Erin and I tried to diagnose each one.

"Holy cow! Look at that bay. Looks like they dunked him in baby oil," I said as I admired the rich sheen of the leggy horse's coat.

"If Pacer shined like that, he'd look like motor oil with hooves." We laughed at her comparison and focused back on the trot out area to watch the big bay move.

"Oh, he's definitely right hind."

"You think? I was watching left front."

We volleyed our opinions back and forth and didn't stop to notice when a man wearing green scrubs walked in until he sat down at our table and set his Diet Mountain Dew bottle on my newly claimed desk.

"Hey there. Which one of you is Amber?" Green Scrubs asked after introducing himself as Dr. Hopper.

"It's me. Hey." I didn't know what else to say, so I just reached out my hand to shake his.

"So what's going on?"

Erin acted intently interested, though the story I rambled out was one she'd heard a million times before. Dr. Hopper, a first-timer to the story, patiently listened to a full account of the previous ten months. He didn't interrupt, didn't look at me like I was crazy, and only took his eyes off mine long enough to reach between my computer screen and Erin's for his bottle of green caffeine.

"We'll know something soon," Dr. Hopper assured me. "He'll be going into X-ray first to make sure his foot is metal-free, and then he'll head over to MRI. Don't worry and don't hesitate to make yourselves comfortable." While grinning at us, he breezed out of the client-lounge-turned-Amber's-office as smoothly as he'd come in.

For the next hour, our computer screens sat blank and e-mails went unanswered as we sipped fresh coffee and filled the lounge's silence with our expert opinions—right front, left hind, right front, right hind.

Green Scrubs stormed back in. His eyes were on fire with excitement. Dr. Hopper motioned for us to come with him. "Follow me. I know your horse's problem."

"You did an X-ray between the ears?" I asked. Erin jabbed me in the ribs as we walked toward radiology.

"No. Better," Dr. Hopper answered. This much animation wasn't something I wanted to see from a vet, especially while he was diagnosing my horse.

We walked through the automatic double doors and were blasted with the smell of sterility. It was clean, cool, and oh so organized. We followed Dr. Hopper around the corner and into the radiology offices. Computer screens lined the walls along with chairs on rollers and a few scattered diet Mountain Dew bottles. The technology seemed so out of place only a corridor away from so many horses but at the same time seemed so perfect.

"Over here." Dr. Hopper gestured to a computer in the far left corner. "He's up on the screen. Do you see it?" His excitement over finding Marquise's needle in a haystack was lost in my inability to read an X-ray. The only thing I noticed for sure was the big black spot where it was supposed to be white.

"What am I looking at?"

"You see the black spot in P1?" Dr. Hopper pointed to make sure I hadn't missed the obvious.

"The thing that looks like a peanut? What is it?"

"It's a subchondral bone cyst and the biggest one I've seen by far."

"Well, that's not exactly comforting. What's it mean?"

"See the tiny defect in the horizontal plane of P1? From it, synovial fluid from the joint leaked into the bone, degraded the tissue, and created a fluid-filled cyst. It's been growing slowly over time. When you exercise Marquise, the fluid pressurizes, and—*boom*—he's lame."

"In English?"

"Your horse has a hole in his leg."

"Oh! So now what?"

"Surgery. I've done several of these with a lot of success, and there's a good chance he'll be able to get back to work."

"Surgery?" This wasn't in my plan for sure. I just wanted to know why Marquise was lame. I never thought there would be a way to fix it.

"We can't do the surgery tomorrow. After today's MRI, it would be too soon, but Wednesday for sure. If all goes well, you can head back home on Thursday."

It was all too much for me, so Erin picked up the line of questioning where I was left speechless. Before I knew it, she and I were walking back to our makeshift office. Her shocked chatter flitted past my ears, and it wasn't until *that* conversation with Jeff that reality sank in.

Marquise had to have surgery.

Wednesday morning the alarm went off at six a.m. With the hotel's blackout curtains drawn, I lay there in the dark and reminisced about the first time I slipped the purple and black halter my dad had given me over Marquise's ears. Though I couldn't remember exactly why, my dad had given the halter to me before I even had a horse. I guess it was just his sweet way of supporting me. On that first day, Marquise's golden forelock glistened in contrast to it, and though a chestnut in purple tack wasn't what I considered fashionable, my horse was perfect.

Today my perfect horse was having surgery, and I couldn't do anything about it. Without surgery there was no chance he'd be okay. We'd battle inconsistent lameness until the pain robbed him of his quality of life. With surgery there was a chance he *might* be okay.

The minutes ticked by, and I finally got up. Erin rolled over, yawned, and sleepily dragged herself out of bed and toward the shower. The gurgle of the coffee pot signaled my final reason to get up, and I poured myself a cup—strong and black, just the way I like it. I reached for my Bible and out of habit turned to Hebrews 11—the faith chapter.

I read it over and over and over. By the time Erin emerged from the shower, clouds of steam in tow, tears were pouring down my face.

"Faith," I said through crying-induced hiccups. "What should I have faith about?"

"What does it say in the first verse?"

"It says we should have confidence in what we hope for and be certain of what we don't see."

"Well?"

"I'm confident that I hope Marquise gets better, and I'm certain I don't know if he will."

"You're missing it," she said. "See this through God's eyes. He wants you to have confidence in His love and know that it's okay to hope for Marquise's soundness. We can't see His plan right now, and we don't know if your horse will ever be sound again. What we do know is that when you trust Him, God will let your experience touch other people. His plan will always bring glory to Him if we let it, so rather than focusing on this as an end to your plans for the trail, try to look at it as the beginning of whatever God has in store for you and Marquise."

Erin was right. God would be glorified, and I had to believe that what I thought was the last chapter of our story would become the first in its sequel.

> Now faith is confidence in what we hope for and assurance about what we do not see.
>
> ### Hebrews 11:1

42

The Dance

After one year post-op, my little redhead was feeling spry again—running around the pasture like his tail was on fire. From one corner of black fence rails to another, Marquise galloped, slowing at the last moment to engage his hips in a sliding stop and blow hard. Standing tall with his chest fully expanded and arching his neck dramatically, his pause was only long enough to draw in a full breath. Once reenergized, he began a high-stepping, show-off routine complete with his fancy Arabian tail wrapped up and over his rump like a decorative Persian rug.

Arn and Ole headed for the barn. Their awkward legs were nowhere near capable of escaping the screaming crimson mass that had thundered past them twice already. Goat safety was never in the forefront of Marquise's mind when he was in one of these moods.

Erin, Pacer, and I enjoyed the performance.

"I don't think you need to have Dr. Woodaman do a lameness exam." Erin's words rang as true as the pounding of Marquise's hooves racing past the fence where she stood grooming Pacer. "Do you think you'll ever do a ride on him again?"

I laughed. "He looks good, doesn't he? I'd love to, but I just don't know that I'd feel right taking him out with that big cyst in his leg. Now if he stays this sound and the cyst fills in...I don't know. Maybe." I rested my chin on my forearms that were crossed over the top rail of the fence and squinted against the June sun. Cherished times like this made me care less that my shirt was getting streaked with the residue of fading fence stain. "All I *really* need is for him to be comfortable."

"Well, friend, it looks to me like you got comfortable and then some, but you'd better put a stop to the craziness and get him cooled off before the vet gets here."

"Agreed." I looped the old brown halter over my shoulder and opened the gate to the pasture. Lucky for me the last ten minutes of top speed sprints took a bit of the wind from Marquise's sails. He was ready to let me slip the rope halter over his nose and tie it at his left cheek while he nibbled the pocket of my shorts for hidden peppermints.

"You're gross, buddy." My hand slid down his sweaty neck and stopped to pat his shoulder. "I don't think Dr. Woodaman is going to be very happy about seeing you like this, especially since she thinks you should be the president of the Cute Pony Club. Right about now the water hose has your name on it."

Marquise's ears didn't indicate he was listening or even cared about what sort of bath was in store for him. They were pricked and pointed straight forward as he nosed around my hip and intently tried to get at those treats.

Some cold water, fly spray, and mane detangler later, a big silver F-350 entered my top pasture. "So how's everybody at Marquise Farms?" Dr. Woodaman asked as she began unpacking her official veterinary stuff.

"It's good," Erin answered. "Pacer's due for shots, and I'd like to do an X-ray or two to see how his feet are coming along with this new shoeing job."

"Sure. And Marquise?"

I heard the question from a few feet away where Marquise had his nose buried in a mass of clover. "I'd like to do an X-ray on him too. There's this knot on the front of Marquise's right hind pastern, and I'd like to know what it is. It doesn't seem to bother him, but I just don't think it looks right."

"Is he lame?" Dr. Woodaman asked.

Erin and I exchanged smiles and knowing glances. "Nope. In fact he just gave us quite an exhibition before you got here, but you know Marquise. If that knot can possibly be something bizarre, it will be."

"You're right about that, and while I'm here, I want a picture of that cyst. I'm just curious what it looks like after a year."

Between the three of us, it only took a few minutes to set up the digital X-ray equipment and get the horses ready. When Pacer was done with his exam, I trotted Marquise straight and on a circle both ways so he could once again show off his soundness.

"He looks good," Dr. Woodaman remarked. "Now let's look at the inside of that leg."

Marquise stepped onto the two-inch wooden block like a circus pony and stood as still as a picture. The X-ray beam settled onto the pastern of his post-surgical leg, and the machine hummed as the digital file uploaded onto the laptop screen. Our three heads circled around as we shielded the sun's glare with our hands. For a moment we forgot that there were three people, $85,000 worth of machinery, and one very proud, redhead locked into one very tiny twelve-by-twelve-foot stall. All we cared about was what the screen had to say.

White contrast of solid bone stood out against a black background, and six eyes trained on the area of the cyst searched for its dark gray void. What we saw was the jagged teeth of the two lag screws that had held the bone together and a spiderweb of new calcification. The cyst was at least ninety-five percent filled in.

"Wow." I'm not sure who said it first, but I do know it came out of each of our mouths at least once. Erin cut her eyes at me. I knew they were asking the question about our future again, but I was too taken aback by what I was seeing to answer it. Would I be able to compete again?

"That looks great," Dr. Woodaman said as she pointed to the screen. Her finger traveled over the joint space and hovered near the lightened area. "I'm just shocked that he's done so well. This is more than you expected, isn't it?"

I nodded. It was. It was more than I had hoped for or even considered. Sure I had prayed for it, but I'd also accepted that a full recovery might never happen. Now I was looking at visual proof that validated the pasture performance. My boy was back.

"It's certainly awesome, but let's have a look at that hind foot." She returned her attention to Marquise and used her hand to follow the curve of his hock down past his knee, cannon, and fetlock before it rested on the suspicious knot where she pressed, pinched, and poked. "It doesn't seem to bother him, does it?"

"No. I just want to know what it is."

"Well, then let's have a look. Go ahead and hop that boy back up on the block."

Marquise obliged. He willingly shifted his weight from one hoof to the other as we jacked up his back end and held him quiet as the X-ray machine did its work and delivered the verdict.

The six eyes that reveled in the glory of the machine's good news moments ago, now became serious. Ringbone.

The rest of the day dragged on. I spent the majority of it in front of the computer researching the degenerative bone condition. The joy I'd felt earlier as I watched Marquise blast around the pasture dissolved. Even though absolutely nothing had changed, with one X-ray *everything* had changed.

⚬⚬⚬⚬⚬

"So what've you learned?" Erin asked the next day when she called to check on my mental state.

"There's no way to fix it. Looks like we made it over one hurdle just to face-plant right into the next one. I should just give up on Marquise and start looking for another horse. Shoot. Maybe I should just give up on horses altogether." I was bummed and believed I sure had a right to be.

"You really think that's going to make it all better?"

"It might. Couldn't make it any worse, could it?"

"I'm sorry. I could have sworn we were outside yesterday watching that horse of yours bolt around the pasture like a fool. Did he look to you like a horse that was ready for you to give up on him? Did he look like he was ready for retirement or that he wanted you to get another horse so he can just sit around and wait for the ringbone to cripple him?"

"No, but I certainly can't ride him."

"I didn't hear the vet say that. Did you?"

"No. She said to go ahead and ride him as long as he was comfortable, and then she made all those other recommendations."

"So she said ride."

"Yes."

"And you don't want to? Why?"

"What if it hurts him? What if it makes it worse? What if he'll stay sounder longer if I just leave him alone?" I was regressing to that state where I worried just for the sake of having something to worry about.

"Amber, what do you think is going to give Marquise the most happiness? Living out his days in a pasture with a couple of half-crazy goats or continuing to get out there to explore the trails and find adventure with his best friend? I'm betting that even without being able to compete again, he'll want to get out there and be needed."

Erin was right—not only about me and Marquise but also about life. Is it possible that we sometimes rob ourselves of today's opportunities to touch lives and experience adventures because we're too worried about our future and what lies ahead of us?

I don't know about you, but I love an old saddle. The question is how can a new saddle become an old one if we're intent on protecting it? In five years and if it stays covered up in the tack room, it might have some dry rot and mold, but with a little bit of oil it will look practically brand new. Or…

In five years you can look back on what was once a slippery, stiff, new saddle and run your fingers over the long scratch across its pommel where your friend's horse balked at a creek crossing and ran you into a tree. You can look at the chewed corner of a stirrup where your dog decided to have a snack while you napped under a tree halfway through a trail ride. You can hold in your hand the few strands of mane that stays clipped to that now old saddle in memory of the trail partner who broke it in for you.

Are you going to quit living today because you want to protect and preserve your future? I decided not to. Marquise and I are going to hit the trail again—albeit a little slower—and I'm going to cherish the last beautiful steps of our dance.

My Wonderful Veterinarians

*Without you
Marquise and I never would have made it back to the trail.
I sincerely value each one of you.*

DR. SCOTT HOPPER
Rood and Riddle Equine Hospital
Lexington, KY
www.roodandriddle.com

❧

DR. RICHARD METCALF
Tryon Equine Hospital
Columbus, NC
www.tryonequine.com

❧

DR. BRYANT PHILLIPS
Cleveland Park Animal Hospital
Travelers Rest, SC
www.clevelandparktr.com

❧

DR. KRISTINE WOODAMAN
Integrated Veterinary Healing
Columbus, NC

The American Endurance Ride Conference
www.aerc.org

Most of the stories in this book happened while Marquise and I were on the trail pursuing the love of a sport called "endurance riding." In a nutshell endurance is long-distance horse racing across varied terrain and often in the most horrible weather imaginable—truly a sport that tests one's mettle and horsemanship.

As in many equestrian sports, the horse's physical condition is judged throughout the event, and its health lies in the capable hands of the rider. Within the endurance community, significant value is placed not only on the immediate but also the long-term physical and emotional well-being of a competitive horse.

The goals of riders vary in endurance riding. Some compete to win or top ten while others pursue mileage goals that accumulate over the years. Still others, and this is the category I fall into, compete simply to explore new trails, spend time camping with friends, and strengthen the bond with their horses.

No matter the goal, we each adhere to the motto of the American Endurance Ride Conference (AERC), which is: "To finish is to win." Being able to cross the finish line with a healthy, sound horse and look forward to the next ride is a satisfying accomplishment and one to be proud of.

I would be honored if you and your horse choose to join us on the trail. I'll be back there soon!

May your trail be happy and your horse always be sound,

Amber and Marquise

AERC Mission Statement

To promote the sport of endurance riding and to encourage and enforce the safe use of horses in demonstrating their endurance abilities in a natural setting through the development, use and preservation of trails. Further, AERC's mission is to maintain horse and ride records of event competition and completions, to record and provide awards to outstanding horses and riders, to ensure that all sanctioned events are conducted in a safe, fair and consistent manner, and to actively promote and conduct educational efforts and research projects that will foster a high level of safety and enjoyment for all horses and riders. The above is to be accomplished with the understanding that goals for the rider must be meshed with the abilities of the horse. Part of AERC's mission is to attract and reward members who act to insure the highest priority for their horses' immediate and long-term physical and emotional health and well-being.